MOTIVATION FOR MINISTRY

SOLI DEO GLORIA

Perspectives
for Every Pastor

Nathan R. Pope

NORTHWESTERN PUBLISHING HOUSE
Milwaukee, Wisconsin

Library of Congress Card 93-83588
Northwestern Publishing House
1250 N. 113th St., Milwaukee, WI 53226-3284
© 1993 by Northwestern Publishing House.
Published 1993
Printed in the United States of America
ISBN 0-8100-0417-8

TABLE OF CONTENTS

Part One:
The Theology of Soli Deo Gloria

Part Two:
A Practical Theology for Soli Deo Gloria

FOREWORD

There was a time when no one resigned from the ministry. Or so it seemed. The only ones who left the ministry were those who were "asked" to resign "for cause."

Times have changed. Ministers are resigning their calls in unprecedented numbers, and many of those who remain—says one survey after another—face discouragement and burnout. In fact, you can find any number of books on the peculiar form of burnout which has afflicted the clergy in the past two decades. Each of them was written by an expert. Each of them offers advice.

This book, *Motivation for Ministry*, also offers advice, but I have not written a manual on the subject of burnout per se. Rather, this is a book by a parish pastor to his fellow parish pastors about basic attitudes. Having once resigned a call, and having had my share of both discouragement and successes, it seemed good to me to present both halves of this pastoral equation from a theological and practical perspective, tracing how the prime directive of giving God the glory affects our attitudes to ministry.

Accordingly, I have entitled my work, *Motivation for Ministry: Soli Deo Gloria* (to God alone the glory). As you read it, please accent the word *soli*, for I believe that this basic, fundamental attitude of wanting to glorify God alone spells the difference between a discouraged or a successful pastor. This holds true no matter how overworked or unappreciated the pastor himself may feel. In other words, I am convinced that the problem facing ministers today is not one of a mutated ministry grown too difficult to handle; no, rather, the problem is one of *attitude*.

So this book constitutes a call to view modern pastoral duties and motives from the ancient perspective of worship as formulated by St. Paul, "So whether you eat or drink or whatever you do, do it all for the glory of God" (1 Corinthians 10:31). I am convinced this worshipful perspective propelled St. Paul to ministerial excellency in spite of the terrific hardships he encountered.

Case histories that illustrate the problems, issues, and peculiarities of the parish ministry are liberally sprinkled throughout this work. They involve my personal experiences as well as those of other pastors. I have taken the liberty to change names and alter circumstances slightly in these stories to ensure anonymity, while at the same time preserving the essence of these cases of casuistry. *Soli Deo Gloria*.

This book is affectionately dedicated to the preparatory, collegiate, and seminary training system of the Wisconsin Evangelical Lutheran Synod for its patient and priceless instruction of me, and to my wife, Patrice, for her patient encouragement of me.

CHAPTER 1
INTRODUCTION

You Don't Quit
Even If Your Orange Crate Breaks

In one eye-opening episode of "The Bob Newhart Show" Bob Hartley reminisced about his childhood minister. Wistfully he told his wife Emily, "I remember sitting there in this big pew, looking up at our minister towering over me in the pulpit and hearing his rich, resonant voice booming out at me. I thought he was God."[1]

In time Dr. Bob came to understand that his minister measured up considerably shorter than God: "Later on, I found out he was only a five foot three inch person standing on an orange crate, speaking through a microphone."[2]

He went on to tell Emily, "One Sunday, in the middle of the sermon, his orange crate collapsed . . . but as he fell through it, he grabbed the microphone. He disappeared behind the lectern, but he kept right on talking. He must have been thrashing around behind there for ten, fifteen minutes, Emily. And he never missed a word of his sermon. And when he pulled himself back up, just in time to say 'Amen,' we all gave him a standing ovation. I'll never forget that, Emily. The man never gave up . . . *I guess that's the way I look at the ministry. You don't quit even if your orange crate breaks.*"[3] So while Bob Hartley's discovery troubled his youthful mind, it also proved helpful. When his minister fell into trouble, Hartley caught sight of his minister's true stature.

Fiction Rooted in Fact

Bob Hartley's view of his minister as one who always tramples defeat underfoot and rises to the occasion with aplomb comes off as a comic-fiction ideal. However, in real life this idealized version of a parish pastor also finds many subscribers. I can supply you with names of those who harbor such stereotypes, and I'm sure you could also add to the list.

Parishes are loaded with people who entertain, what Edward Bratcher terms, an inflated opinion of their ministers. Bratcher served as a parish pastor for many years and later as a consultant to The Southern Baptist Theological Seminary. He, too, watched the episode of "The Bob Newhart Show" in which Bob Hartley idolized his boyhood pastor. His book for ministers, *The Walk-on-Water Syndrome*, fairly howls in protest over such a characterization: "The choice to use this issue—the superhuman nature of ministers—as the basis for a popular TV show indicates the *prevalence* of such an attitude. The writers assumed, and I believe correctly, that the average TV viewer would understand the setting and would also laugh at the ridiculous attitude which is *normally* held."[4]

While I am willing to agree with Bratcher that the superhuman nature of ministers exists in theory only, I also know that parishioners want to set their ministers on pedestals

and picture them as immune to the ordinary sins which beset other mortals. And no amount of complaining on the
part of the clergy will change that perception. Someone has
already said it: perception is reality.

It's rather amazing that public expectations for the Christian ministry overall remain high despite the image problems which the sins of some clergy have created. Recent sex
and money scandals, for example, have demonstrated the
ordinary, less than superhuman nature of many televangelists, ministers, and priests. Many of these reports sensation-
alized clergy sins and shenanigans in a style nothing short of
uproarious. How some have greeted these scandals with glee
troubles me.

Nevertheless, public expectations for the Christian ministry remain amazingly high. Organized religion, according
to a September 1988 Gallup poll, surfaced as the institution
Americans most trusted.

Why does the public place such a high trust in and expect such great things from the Christian ministry despite
the revelations of ministers who have fallen from their
pedestals with such thuds? Is the public's attitude toward
the Christian ministry illogical? Unrealistic? I choose to believe that the word *hopeful* best explains the attitude of the
public. I would maintain that Bob Hartley's never-say-quit
minister represents the ideal which many people, church
people especially, hope and expect the Christian minister
will live up to. Yes, I'm well aware that ministers can complain about this expectation. But I would also argue that
ministers should accept this ideal as a reality and then seek
to understand why people persist in thinking as they do. My
own experience over the years teaches me that parishioners
idealize their ministers for good reason.

I believe that Bob Hartley's idealized minister is not rooted in fiction but is, indeed, based on fact. The idealized
minister, the man who keeps going even when his orange

crate breaks, exists. His counterpart exists in the great personalities of the Bible and of history, in the lives of lesser men, and most prominently in the person of Jesus Christ. These four sources contribute to what I call the *hopeful ideal* of ministry.

Scriptural Counterparts

Do you think it unrealistic or exaggerated to idealize the ministry a la Bob Hartley? If so, have you considered the fact that the Bible itself has contributed to what some may see as this caricature of the heroic minister?

The Bible parades before its readers columns of dedicated ministers, marching like an army through the sacred story. Their exploits sound more like fiction than fact. I think especially about the appalling conditions under which many of these dedicated saints of old labored. These Biblical heroes fed on the food of adversity. Their level of commitment shines through clearly, especially when it is contrasted against the ugly backdrop of their difficulties and heartaches. Their willingness and ability to do their work under extremely trying conditions, to my mind, gives a partial definition to what we might call ministerial competency: they refused to give up.

Moses steered a nation of whiners to the promised land, reaping even his family's open rebellion along the way. Elijah, in one sense, was his age's Rodney Dangerfield; from his defeated enemies he could get no respect. Jeremiah found himself the target of death threats when his incisive sermons calling for repentance turned a crowd of clergy and laity into a mob. Hosea married Gomer, a woman of questionable morals, to dramatize Israel's apostasy. Amos was charged with conspiracy and threatened with death. John the Baptist suffered censure, imprisonment, and decapitation. Paul of Tarsus lived through a whole catalog of sufferings, experiencing everything from political intrigues to sinking ships. And Rome banished the Apostle John to Patmos.

The staying power of the prophets and apostles under such severe conditions reveals itself as dramatic, heroic, and humbling. Luther, himself a frequent victim of and victor over hardships, had to admit: "I am angry with myself and am ashamed of myself and my life. I regret that after the manifestation of Christ we pay such cold attention to our gifts and believe the Word so feebly. Yet the fathers believed with such great constancy . . . compared with them, we are cold and sleepy amid the abundance and the great glory of the manifestation of Christ."[5]

Bible readers know full well how it portrays the ministry within its pages. The ministers of the Bible, "faced jeers and flogging, while still others were chained and put in prison. They were stoned; they were sawed in two; they were put to death by the sword. They went about in sheepskins and goatskins, destitute, persecuted, and mistreated—the world was not worthy of them. They wandered in deserts and mountains, and in caves and holes in the ground (Hebrews 11:36-38).[6]

Comparisons, therefore, of what was once to what is now are inevitable. Every minister will be measured by the biblical ideal; the comparisons prove themselves inescapable. The present day minister who would pick up the prophet's mantle cannot escape the prophet's shadow.

Historical Counterparts

You can also trace the *hopeful ideal* of the Christian minister to the testimonies of church history. Great men leave behind great legacies; denominational heroes create for would-be disciples an historical ideal. I think of Luther and Chemnitz and American Lutherans like Walther and the brothers Pieper, to name a few; they shape my version of the historical ideal. Luther Rice, Spurgeon, and many others form this ideal for Baptists. Episcopalians think of Cranmer, Trench, and Seabury. Methodists have the Wesleys and Whitefield, while Presbyterians look to Calvin, Knox, and Beza. Every denomination of the Christian Church numbers its great men as contributors to the historical ideal of ministry. Every minister of the Christian Church, consequently, eventually feels himself inextricably compared to the standards of his denomination's stellar performers.

Lesser Counterparts

More than likely the hopeful ideal of ministry exists in every community. It was my incomparable professor of English at Northwestern College, the late Dr. Elmer Kiessling, who confirmed this truth in a way that I have never forgotten. He had us Juniors reading Geoffrey Chaucer's *Canterbury Tales* in the original old English, an initially trying task, but one which we came to enjoy because the characters and the stories proved so engaging and unforgettable, and the studies in human nature proved so timeless.

One pilgrim on the way to Canterbury, the priest, impressed me more than any other. Since I was involved in preministerial studies, the character of the priest hit home, and it stayed with me long after I had exiled my copy of *Canterbury Tales* to the attic. I hope you might share my enthusiasm for the character sketch of the man whom Geoffrey Chaucer described as the quintessential model of ministerial competency. He paints an affectionate portrait of him: "There was a good man of the church, a poor parish priest, but rich in holy thoughts and works. He was also a learned man, a cleric, who wished to preach Christ's gospel truly and to teach his parishioners devoutly. He was benign, wonderfully diligent, and extremely patient in adversity, as he had proved many times."[7]

Poor, overworked, and unrecognized, Chaucer's anonymous parson ministered competently, working like a true shepherd. "He was a pastor and not a mercenary. And yet, though he himself was holy and virtuous, he was not contemptuous of sinners, nor overbearing and proud in his talk; rather he was discreet and kind in his teaching. His business was to draw folk to heaven by fairness and by setting a good example."[8]

Chaucer's parish pastor labored in obscurity, preaching and living the gospel. He set a standard for others—a standard which Chaucer recognized and recorded. Chaucer's praiseworthy description of the priest fits men I have personally encountered as well as others whose worthy reputations I have learned about. Often, when I pull on my robes and mount the pulpit and face a sea of faces, a feeling wells up in me which says: "I'm standing in a pulpit once occupied by other men whose work and dedication give meaning to the term pastor, whose sermons are still bearing fruit, and whose expertise won them recognition as men of character, and boy, I had better measure up." I admit I enjoy the thrill of the challenge, and I wonder whether others have ever experienced that same sensation and how they have dealt with it. Chaucer ended his description of the priest by saying, "I don't believe there is a better priest anywhere. He cared nothing for pomp and reverence, nor did he affect an overly nice conscience; he taught the lore of Christ and his twelve apostles, but first he followed it himself."[9]

Do Chaucer's glowing words describe the minister who preceded you in your present charge, or do they fit the man who inspired you to enter the ministry? Do they also become you? You and I certainly enjoy models of the hopeful ideal of ministry both in the ranks of our predecessors and among our contemporary colleagues. May you and I aspire to be numbered among them as well.

The Christlike Counterpart

We all, of course, recognize Christ as the ideal minister. We also identify his attitude as the one forming the essence of pastoral competency: he became less than he was to serve sinners. Humility marks the spirit of Christ because, even though he was the Son of God, he stooped to serve. Paul says of Christ that he "made himself nothing, taking the very nature of a servant, being made in human likeness. And being found in appearance as a man, he humbled himself and became obedient to death—even death on a cross" (Philippians 2:7,8)!

As ministers of Christ, you and I wish to become less than what we are to serve others in his name. This means we can never escape the inevitable comparisons to the Christ who humbled himself. I can see no other way around it. If you and I are to grow in competency as ministers, then we must be willing to calibrate all of our attitudes by the standard which guided Christ—humility.

The portrayal of Chaucer's priest shows a man whose ministerial habits were patterned after those of Christ. And, interestingly enough, you will find the antithesis of this spirit in Chaucer's characterization of the friar, another clergyman who made the trip to Canterbury. Chaucer says he was "a wanton, merry friar, a licensed beggar and a very gay man. . . . He heard confession very agreeably, and his absolution was pleasant. When he thought he would get a good present, he was an easy man in giving penance. . . . He knew the taverns well in every town, and cared more for every innkeeper and barmaid than for a leper or a beggar. . . . And, above everything, wherever there was a chance for profit, this friar was courteous and humbly helpful. There was no man anywhere more capable at this work."[10]

The friar lacked what the priest possessed, a Christlike disposition. He was for Chaucer what Elmer Gantry is for us. The caricature of the friar, I firmly believe, merely serves to underscore the fact that Christian people instinctively expect that true ministers of God will behave themselves as such. Or let me put it this way. Likeness to Christ constitutes an occupational hazard of the shepherd under Christ; the people we serve expect us to be Christlike and expect us to continue to grow in Christlikeness. No minister who serves the flock as the undershepherd of Christ should then imagine himself as someone who is exempt from the inevitable comparisons to Christ, the flock's Chief Shepherd.

I contend that comparisons to Christ come with the turf. In fact, I find it demeaning to Christ and his church when I hear or read about ministers who complain about their parishioners' expectations of them in such a way that suggests they are all too willing to water down the model their Lord left them. To argue that we must lower the standards of integrity required of ministers today because the times have changed and that present-day men lack the faith and fortitude of a by-gone age to conform to apostolic models of Christlike competency is to denigrate the Christlike model (Titus 1:6-9; 1 Peter 5:1-4). So those who seek to minister in controversy, who demand that people accept their unscriptural divorces or sexual perversions or soul-destroying heresies, certainly are not following the model the Lord left for them.

Rather than complaining or seeking to diminish or whittle down the hopeful ideal of ministry, we, as pastors, have only one choice. That choice is outlined for us in Paul's prayer for the Ephesians: "I pray that out of his glorious riches he may strengthen you with power through his Spirit in your inner being, so that Christ may dwell in your hearts through faith" (Ephesians 3:16,17). You get the picture. It all comes down to faith—a faith created by the Word of God and sustained by it, a faith that promises to keep Christ in the hearts of his children. When you and I feel ourselves buckling under the pressure to conform ourselves to Christlikeness, we will consequently return to the Word. I maintain that the degree to which a shepherd of Christ grazes on the Word and believes it, so in proportion he derives strength in his inner being to model Christ on the outside for all to see. We are only as strong as the food we eat.

Unreal but Perfectly Understandable Expectations

As I have attempted to demonstrate, I believe you can trace the hopeful *ideal* of ministry to a composite picture drawn from Scripture, history, contemporary examples, and Christ. I believe parishioners are justified in entertaining the high standards for their pastors modeled by these four sources.

Yet, it must be noted that parishioners sometimes do harbor expectations of their ministers which fall within the realm of the unreal and of the unfair, yes, even of the ridiculous. Edward Bratcher comments, "The pastor is expected to walk on water, and he cannot, and he becomes angry with himself because he cannot."[11] You and I, like our people, have our limitations. But, we also know that many of our people labor under the delusion that their pastor must possess superhuman powers since he represents God. How this works I will demonstrate in the following formula: Christ is omniscient; therefore Christ's ministers can also be expected to be omniscient, that is, they must somehow manage to know what remains hidden to ordinary mortals. Yes, some people actually think this way. As evidence consider the following pastor's experience—an experience that is perhaps somewhat similar to one that you've shared.

"Pastor, my sister was in the hospital all week, and you didn't come to visit her," said the parishioner. He was elderly, red-faced, and upset. He had invaded the quiet of the sacristy five minutes before the beginning of the worship service, and he stood towering over the seated minister.

"I was telling my friends yesterday night at the card game what kind of pastors we have, and they thought it was terrible." His lips quivered as his words rose in anger.

"Why did you wait until Saturday to complain to your friends? Why didn't you call me during the week and let me know—I didn't know," responded the frustrated pastor.

"Come on!" protested the parishioner, unconvinced. He wheeled on his heels and blew out of the sacristy, while the tolling of the bell reminded the pastor that the time had arrived for the service to begin.

It's maddening, I know, at times to hear your limited attributes confused with Christ's attributes. Sometimes you don't know what to do—laugh or cry.

I also think of what happens when parishioners expect you to duplicate the abilities of your predecessors. Some people take it for granted that your predecessor's talents will be transferred to you somehow, a la Elisha inheriting Elijah's spirit (2 Kings 2:9,10), when you pick up the cloak of succession.

As many have discovered upon entering a new charge, the tribute Chaucer penned for his parson can likewise be inked, with both admiration and exaggeration, on the memory of a recently departed predecessor. Perhaps you know from experience how hard it can be to follow in the footsteps of a man who served a parish with distinction. The hopeful ideal of ministry can be distressing to the minister who finds himself haunted by the ghost of a predecessor's competency, especially if it is a grossly inflated one.

I suspect that frustration and anger are the normal reactions to these unreal expectations. While the grinding and gnashing of teeth describes hell's peculiar sounding music, does it not also find a toothy chorus among ministers who grow resentful of their parishioners' expectations?

I would caution that this sort of parishioner expectation and confusion comes with the territory. People have put together their ideals of what ministers are supposed to be like for a reason. The model of Christ the Good Shepherd has had something to do with this, and so have the models of those competent, Christlike servants who have gone before us and in whose footsteps you and I are now walking. So when you encounter expectations which strike you as unreal, grant yourself a measure of peace by understanding why people entertain them. Instead of automatically responding to these unreal expectations as criticisms or insults or putdowns, train yourself to recognize these expectations as compliments. Recognize these unrealistic hopes as forms of praise—that people would think us worthy in the first place to be included with such lofty predecessors!

Of Majors, Minors, and Motives

Written a generation ago, the *Christian Minister's Manual* contains a timeless bit of advice for today's minister: "Conscious that he is the representative of Christ and his church, the minister should look, speak, act, and live the part."[12]

The minister's "part" actually contains many parts. The typical pastor of a parish is called upon to perform many distinct and varied duties. (You may want to page ahead briefly to pages 96 and 97 and locate there an impressive list of thirty pastoral activities which were compiled by one expert.)

Managing these parts, allowing each of them ample time, prioritizing them—this, I would say, points to yet another definition of competency. Some ministers, in managing their many pastoral duties, seem artfully able to steer a course around the obstacles which block competency. Others seem doomed to lurch about, to crash against the obstacles, and eventually to career out of control pell-mell. Do those who fail attempt too much? Do those who succeed attempt too little?

Failure and success in managing pastoral duties can, of course, be traced to the abilities a person possesses. However, I also believe that this involves more than just native talents. In fact, I hope to demonstrate that motives, correct ones, keep ministers going when programs and goals crash under their feet or, conversely, when they succeed past their wildest dreams. How this involves the glory of God you might well imagine, but I will leave no room for speculation as this introductory chapter draws to a close.

The Ministerial Menu

"The sermon ought to receive the top spot on his [the minister's] weekly list of priorities," say Schuetze and Habeck, authors of *The Shepherd under Christ,* a Lutheran textbook for pastoral theology.[13] A statement like this, loaded with code words such as "top," "weekly," "list," and especially "priorities," should be interpreted by novices, like seminarians, to mean that the ministry promises more than sermons. Until they actually become settled in parish life, seminarians possess little inkling of just how many priorities they will encounter in the ministry; the inkling, when it comes, is often unsettling. The duties of the typical parish pastor spread before him such an array of possibilities that they are guaranteed to create mixed sensations in him. It's like being in the situation where the waitress hands you a menu so thick with possibilities that you're unable to decide what to order first; you want to eat, but you don't know where to start. "Truly," say Schuetze and Habeck, "being a pastor is a many-sided assignment."[14]

The Jack-of-all-trades

In my role as a parish pastor I see myself as an ecclesiastical handyman, a general practitioner. I do much more than preach. The great Baptist professor of homiletics, John Broadus, puts it this way: "The Christian minister is not

only a preacher; he is also a teacher, a pastor; an administrator, a counselor, a community servant, and perhaps other
things."[15]

What are some of the "other things" you and I might do?
Well, our parish responsibilities may see us doing, in turn,
the work of a missionary, author/publisher, public relations
director, fund raiser, or worship leader. And so it continues
until you could easily compile a list of 30 or more possible
pastoral activities. So think of yourself as a general practitioner of spiritual medicine rather than as a specialist. In
fact, it's my opinion that some of the burnout problems of
ministers can be traced to a misunderstanding of the *general*
nature of the parish ministry. Some men want to specialize
in every facet of the profession—but the day contains only
so many hours.

Musts and Maybes

The ministry involves duties which a minister *must* do
and others which he *may* do, that is, if he has the time. In
other words, both majors and minors fill his agenda, and
temptations to major in the minors or to treat the majors as
minors never die.

The temptation to neglect certain ministerial duties can
sometimes be chalked up to the special gifts a minister possesses. Conscientiousness, or for that matter even ignorance, can cause a man to major in his strengths and to minor in his weaknesses. Gifted with a talent for chumminess,
a minister, for example, may want to specialize in a ministry
of visitation or public relations while his pulpit and admin-
istrative duties become, as it were, brides left at the altar.
The parish minister, by his call, finds himself married, not
only to the loves of his ministry, but also to those he finds a
lot less desirable.

Scholarship can also throw the delicate equilibrium between ministerial majors and minors out of kilter. Seminar-

ies try to be practical. Some succeed more than others. Still, the ivory tower of scholarship casts its long shadows of theory over the best of classrooms, and some students develop uncompromising mentalities towards the inevitable clash between theory and reality—the parish ministry. Bratcher admits that his college and seminary experience turned him into a specialist. With the mind of a specialist he approached the varied menu of his ministerial duties and found himself unprepared for the shock of reality. He says he felt incompetent to deal with the all the things he was supposed to do.

Pursuing the Ideal

"He's not cut out for the ministry," the man admitted. His son had just dropped out of ministerial training, and he was explaining the situation to his family pastor. "The ministry is a tough row to hoe," the father said ruefully.

Add the ideal of what a minister *must be* to the menu of what a minister *must do,* and the resulting combination proves itself more than some can handle. More and more we hear ministers protesting how difficult they have it. More and more we are witnessing resignations in unprecedented numbers. The zeal and dedication with which so many began their ministries evaporates in time like the haze on the horizon.

How can a minister preserve the zeal that led him into the ministry and at the same time combine it with the pragmatism of his experience so that he not only keeps going in his ministry, but also is happy in it? Answer the question with the word motive.

Design for Disaster

Pride is the wrong motive for entering the ministry. Define pride as the sinful desire to advance one's self. Just as pride led to Satan's fall from heaven, so it sinks ministries.

Paul wrote to Timothy about guarding against pride: "He [the minister] must not be a recent convert, or he may become conceited and fall under the same judgment as the devil" (1 Timothy 3:6). Notice how Paul connects conceit to Satan's demise. Define ministerial competency then also as the guarding against pride, for to be a minister means to become less than one's self—in the spirit of our Lord who humbled himself in the days of his exinanition—and to advance someone else, namely, God.

Unfortunately, the psyche of some ministers insures that purity of motives will be a never ending battle for them. While the selfless nature of Christ stands as the hopeful ideal for his undershepherds, they in reality often imitate the devilish pride of the god of the underworld.

The ministry, as a profession, exhibits an odd knack for collecting more than its share of pride-filled men. I make this claim on the basis of what I have read and witnessed and experienced. I, for one, have been tempted to advance myself in more sinful ways than I care to tell you about.

Yes, the ministry collects egotistical individuals like a porch light does bugs, not because the holy office creates pride, but because proud men have always been attracted to the power-filled possibilities of the office.[16] So, "Know thyself" becomes advice which aptly applies to ministers and their motives. Ministers need to grapple with the realization that the ministry does attract some power seeking, selfish, anti-social individuals, just as it has always done. And while Eli's sons are long rotted in their graves (1 Samuel 4:10,11), their lascivious and self-centered agendas live on in too many instances. And so it would be foolish to dismiss this psychological profile, which unfortunately fits some.[17]

While the falsely motivated pastor—who, much like one of Eli's sons, surfaces as a marginal or full blown sociopath—is indeed rare, yet, consider the common egotist. He is just as destructive to the parish and to the reputation of the gospel, plying away in his calling with the hope of increasing his own significance. It is not pleasant to contemplate, but it is, nevertheless, true. Some men desperately pursue the hopeful ideal of ministerial competency simply because their jacked-up egos enjoy and want the limelight, prestige, and power that comes with the job.[18]

Lack of humility kills ministries; pride sets ministers up for the big crash. F. LaGard Smith in *Fallen Shepherds, Scattered Sheep* writes that ministers "fall so hard because they have built their pedestals so high."[19] The gospel, with its requisites for holy living, in a sense sets ministers on a pedestal (1 Timothy 6:11; 2 Timothy 2:24; 1 Peter 5:2,3). Pride, however, in the tradition of Babel, wants to build that pedestal still higher.

I wonder if this could help to explain why some men resign from the ministry. Could frustrated plans for self-aggrandizement contribute to a minister's disenchantment with his calling? If pride motivates a man to be the best he can be, I can see the possibility of that individual growing bitter if his parishioners fail to respond to his plans or actions with the praise he was expecting. Now, I am not suggesting that all who quit the ministry do so because their egos got in the way. What I am saying is that you and I must always be attentive to what motivates us to do what we do. And I am promising that we will feel more fulfillment and less bitterness if we always strive to advance God alone in all our pastoral pursuits. Come what may, I make this promise without any qualifications.

The Superseding Motive

Call pride the big, false motive for ministry. But then recognize also that many correct motives for serving Christ and his church obviously do exist. As I pointed out earlier, ministers have an array of duties in their parish work to balance and perform. Each duty demands a corresponding ability.

27

Take counseling as an example. A man with a tender heart wants to help people. And because God has blessed him with that soft and sympathetic heart, he feels drawn to the ministry . God has blessed a second man with a good set of lungs and a gift for gab. He feels led to enter the ministry because he believes he can preach effectively. A third man wants to teach. A fourth wants to evangelize. All of these motives involve personal decisions to use God-given abilities in such a way that they build up the church. All are legitimate for ministry.

Know, however, that one grand and glorious motive exists which supersedes all secondary motives for ministry, one motive alone which gives purpose to the Christian ministry as it also defines the reason for all created existence—the glorification of God. Jay Adams says, "The one overall goal that we must set for everything we do is the glory of God."[20] Adam's assertion can only be understated, never overstated, for Paul wrote to the Corinthians, "Whatever you do, do it all for the glory of God" (1 Corinthians 10:31).

How should the ministry purpose to glorify God? Will the ministry promote God's glory as just one among many glories? Is God's glory to stand preeminent among lesser glories—like Jacob's sheaf of grain standing among the gathered and bowed sheaves of his brothers (Genesis 37:7) or like a feudal lord standing among his vassal barons? Will the ministry seek God's glory while also seeking its own glory?

For the Society of Jesus, which he founded, Ignatius de Loyola coined just one such statement of purpose: maiorem Dei gloriam (for the greater glory of God).[21] Loyola's aim for his Society of Jesus raises the obvious question: whose glory, besides that of God's glory, is to be promoted? Does God's Word command ministers of Christ to pursue a multi-layered plan of glorification? Is God's glory to be shared with any other? Are ministers of God to seek the "greater glory of God" or to seek the "glory of God alone"?

"Whatever you do, do it all for the glory of God" (1 Corinthians 10:31) ultimately limits all motives and purposes of ministry to the glorification of God alone. As its highest ambition, the ministry, by apostolic command, aims to glorify God. Christian ministers then will minister soli Deo gloria (to the glory of God alone). Soli (alone) is the key. The *soli* of soli Deo gloria unlocks the door to ministerial competence and personal happiness—a matter of doctrine and practical theology which I aim to unfold in the pages to come. In my first division I explain the doctrine of God's glory, and in the second I indicate its practical application.

I hope to convince you—to the degree you understand why God is glorified, to the degree you know how God is glorified in your pastoral ministrations, and to the extent you consciously minister with God's glorification as your only goal—that you will experience:

1. A sense of accomplishment,
2. The drive to persevere in your ministry,
3. A heightened sense of dedication,
4. A desire to make personal and professional improvements; and,
5. Personal happiness.

Those who minister soli Deo gloria, I am convinced, won't give up, but will keep on going even when their orange crates break.

Summary

1. Despite screaming headlines about failed ministers, people continue to demand high standards for those who enter the public ministry. People piece together their idealized version of ministers from heroic qualities they have found in biblical saints, denominational giants, average but faithful men, and ultimately Christ himself.

2. The parish pastor faces many duties. Consequently he feels the constant temptation to specialize in those areas which interest him the most or in those areas where he believes his greatest talents lie. The parish pastor, however, is a spiritual generalist. While he may have entered the ministry for a variety of personal reasons, the minister has one superseding goal in his ministry—a goal which gives it eternal purpose, the glorification of God.

3. To the degree that the minister consciously and knowingly seeks to glorify God, he will grow in both professional competency and personal happiness.

4. As I initially define it, pastoral competency means refusing to give up, working like a shepherd, guarding against pride, emulating Christ's spirit of humility, and managing well the major and minor tasks of ministry.

Advice

1. What person has most significantly influenced your style and attitude as a pastor? In what way?

2. Are you currently modeling your ministerial style/ methodology after someone? If not, whom would you choose? Consider making an appointment with a neighboring pastor whose ways and habits you respect. Sit down with him, pick his brains, and learn how he came to excel.

3. List on paper all the duties you perform as a pastor. Using a scale from 1 to 10 (1 being lowest and 10 being highest), grade your duties. Which do you like the best? The worst? Where are your talents the strongest? The weakest? Determine if you need to rearrange your use of time to coincide with your priorities.

4. Do you specialize in areas of your ministry which interest you or complement your character/intellectual strengths?

If so, do you get parishioner feed-back? Do they approve or disapprove?

5. Do you tend to work hardest in areas of your ministry in which you receive the greatest amount of praise from your parishioners or the greatest amount of criticism?

Endnotes

[1] "The Bob Newhart Show," television performance (show #7357), produced by Martin Cohan, CBS, 6 October 1973, script page 48.

[2] Ibid.

[3] Ibid., 49 [Emphasis added].

[4] Edward B. Bratcher, *The Walk-on-Water Syndrome* (Waco, Texas: Word Books, 1984), 23 [Emphasis added].

[5] Ewald Plass, *What Luther Says*, 3 vols. (St. Louis: Concordia Publishing House, 1959), 2:997-98.

[6] The quotation is taken from the *New International Version* (NIV), from which all Scripture citations are taken.

[7] *The Canterbury Tales*, trans. R. M. Lumiansky (New York: Washington Square Press, 1948), 10.

[8] Ibid.

[9] Ibid.

[10] Ibid., 5.

[11] Bratcher, *The Walk-on-Water Syndrome*, 27.

[12] James DeForest Murch, *Christian Minister's Manual* (Cincinnati: Standard Publishing, 1937), 13.

[13] Schuetze and Habeck, *The Shepherd under Christ* (Milwaukee: Northwestern Publishing House, 1974), 14.

[14] Ibid., 19.

[15] John A. Broadus, *On the Preparation and Delivery of Sermons* (San Francisco: Harper and Row, 1979), 6.

[16] See Paul D. Meier, Frank B. Minirth, and Frank Wichern, *Introduction to Psychology and Counseling* (Grand Rapids: Baker Book House, 1982), 223. The authors believe that the ministry attracts anti-social personalities.

[17] See Minirth, Meier, and Wichern, *Introduction to Psychology and Counseling*, 224. The authors document their belief that many ministers are

anti-social through research generated by the Minnesota Multiphase Personality Inventory.

[18] See G. Lloyd Rediger, *Coping with Clergy Burnout* (Valley Forge: Judson Press, 1982), 40. Rediger writes of a dominating characteristic of the clergy towards exhibitionism.

[19] F. LaGard Smith, *Fallen Shepherds Scattered Sheep* (Eugene, Oregon: Harvest House Publishers, 1988), 35.

[20] Jay E. Adams, *Back to the Blackboard* (Phillipsburg, New Jersey: Presbyterian and Reformed Pub. Co., 1982), 22.

[21] See Malachi Martin, *The Jesuits* (New York: Simon and Schuster, 1987), 160, for a description of Loyola's ambitions to play second fiddle to God.

PART ONE

THE THEOLOGY OF SOLI DEO GLORIA

CHAPTER 2: GOD CREATED ALL THINGS FOR HIS GLORY

The Bible's Great Revelation

"Who am I?" and "What am I doing here?" I wondered. No, I wasn't suffering from amnesia, and I wasn't lost. I was a twelve year old schoolboy, and the cause of my astonishment lay in the chance sighting of myself in a mirror.

Classes had let out, and I had hurried to the cloakroom to put on my Safety Patrol belt and badge and the rest of the neat stuff that boys my age, back in the early 60s, used to wear to bring motorists to a halt at the crossing. There I stood, just inside the door, when I happened to look up and spot myself in the mirror which hung overhead. At the sight I suddenly froze and stared. Without warning I had the queerest feeling come over me. The questions popped into my head, "Who am I?" "What am I doing here?"

I will always remember that afternoon meeting with myself, and I have never been quite the same since posing those questions.

Up to that point in my life I had defined my identity pretty well as any adolescent might. I was the son of a loving mother and father. I was an eighth grader, so naturally my position on the Boy's A basketball team was assured. And I had advanced to the position of Lieutenant on the Safety Patrol.

I guess I considered this one of the really big clues to the "who" and "what" of my identity. In my youthful mind it had never dawned on me in any meaningful way that I could define the purpose of my existence on a higher level. You might say that my "mirror experience" marks the point in my life where I took my first adult step at defining my identity philosophically and spiritually. Little did I realize then, when I first began to brood on the purpose of my existence, that all of life and its activities represent godly and evil answers to my two questions.

"Who am I; what am I doing here?" Consciously or otherwise, these questions drive human thinking and activity. I challenge you to trace any human action that comes to your mind—bank robbery, college graduation, marriage, or anything traced to its genesis—and you will confirm the basic nature of this "who" and "what" of human identity.

Of course I am not telling you anything you do not already know. But, by this line of reasoning I hope to emphasize that humankind, without the enlightenment of God's Word, has never been able to get past the "who" and "what" of identity. A mind darkened by sin can raise and ask questions about one's identity but can never fully understand it (1 Corinthians 1:18-20).

Today people spend enormous sums of money attempting to unlock the purpose of their existence through costly psychoanalysis. In order to find the secret to life, some jettison their conventional lives and move to Alaska to take up residence beside a frozen stream. Others aspire to land a profitable fast food franchise and find purpose to life by making money. And a few are simply content to loaf and think the whole matter over at the expense of taxpayers.

In his or her own way each person on earth is ultimately seeking the answer to these questions about existence. For many it remains an unending search because they are looking for the answers in the wrong places. The Bible, however, answers these questions. I mentioned the Bible's solution at the end of the introductory chapter, but I will repeat it: Glorify. Whom? God. Paul wrote, "*Whatever* you do, do it all for the *glory of God*" (1 Corinthians 10:31). Paul's statement succeeds in defining both the immediate and the ultimate issue of human existence and purpose. His use of "whatever" refers to the endless menu of human activities which daily fill every human life. The words "glory of God" define what the ultimate goal of all human activity must aim to do, to glorify the Creator.

The Bible matter of factly makes its claim that humans were created for the ultimate end of glorifying God (Isaiah 43:7). Think of a passage like Psalm 19:l: "The heavens declare the glory of God; the skies proclaim the work of his hands" Or think of Psalm 148 in which the psalmist commands the various levels of creation, the worlds of spirits, humans, lower life forms, and inanimate things, to praise God: "Let them praise the name of the LORD, for he commanded and they were created" (Psalm 148:5).

"Who am I; what am I doing here?" Be it rock, moon, gazelle, angel, man or woman, God created everything, small or big, for the sole purpose of giving him glory through their properties or activities. The Bible not only makes that claim; it also explains how it is to be done. To understand that we must take a look at how the Bible uses the words glory, glorify, and glorification.

The Meaning of the Word "Glory"

The Bible uses twelve different nouns which have been variously understood as the equivalent of the English word "glory." The Old Testament alone uses ten of those synonyms. Of these, I intend to concentrate on the two main words, *kabod* (Hebrew) and *doxa* (Greek).

Kittel, explaining that *kabod* has the essential meaning of "something weighty which gives importance,"[22] says, "In relation to God it [*kabod*] denotes that which makes God impressive."[23]

The Greek word *doxa* continues the sense of *kabod* into the New Testament, even though its etymology differs. The noun *doxa* derives its meaning from *dokeo*, "to think," "to believe." Saying that doxa "most likely signifies one who stands in good repute,"[24] Kittel asserts that *kabod* shaped its basic definition. In usage then, *kabod* and *doxa* mean essentially the same thing. The glory of God means "what God essentially is and does, as exhibited in whatever way he reveals himself in these respects."[25]

God's Glory Versus God's Glorification

I see it as a mistake to think that the glory of God and God's glorification refer to identical things, even though the terms *kabod* and *doxa* appear in both phrases throughout the Bible. God's glory needs to be distinguished from his glorification.

For example, take a look at the phrase "the glory of God." This phrase can mean two things. Edward Young writes, "Theologians have rightly distinguished between God's essential glory, that glory which he has in and of himself as God, and the glory which he has displayed in the created universe."[26] In Psalm 24:9,10 *kabod* refers to the reality of God's essential and unique attributes, all that makes him God: "Lift up your heads, O you gates; lift them up, you ancient doors, that the King of glory [*kabod*] may come in. Who is he, this King of glory? The LORD almighty—he is the King of glory."

In Exodus 16:10, on the other hand, you have an example of how the Bible uses *kabod* in connection with God's self-revelation of his essential being: "While Aaron was speaking to the whole Israelite community, they looked toward the desert, and there was the glory [*kabod*] of the LORD appearing in the cloud."

August Pieper, professor of Semitic languages at Wisconsin Lutheran Seminary for over 40 years, describes how the reality of God's essential glory is distinguished from the glory of his self-revelation: "It [the glory of the LORD] is, to the degree that it is unfolded, a more or less complete image of the true glory, of the absolute and infinite transcendence of God over all creatures according to his all-pervading presence, his all-dominating power, his infinite grace, and his all-consuming holiness—a symbol of his absolute sovereignty, of the one and only true and perfect God, to whom all creatures ought to render willing obeisance and joyful service, and offer adoration, praise, and glory without end."[27]

There you have it. The glory of God means all that comprises God and also how he chooses to reveal it. But, if you look at Pieper's words, you will also notice that in making the distinction between the essential reality of God's glory and God's self-revelation of that glory, the professor also touches upon the definition of glorification. God's glorification refers not to God's "uncovered, unveiled divine perfection of glory,"[28] nor to any supernatural manifestation in which God reveals his presence or power. As Pieper explains, creatures work the glorification of God. To glorify God means to respond to all that makes God glorious.

Think of worship as another name for the glorification of God.

Glorifying God Is Worship

"Ascribe to the LORD the glory due his name" (1 Chronicles 16:29), said David, using the word *kabod*. "Fear God and give him glory" (Revelation 14:7), shouted the apocalyptic angel, using the word *doxa*. Both verses illustrate how the glorification of God sets itself apart from God's essential glory and his supernatural revelations of that glory. Glorification represents creation's response to the totality of God. "Giving God glory means acknowledging (Acts 12:23) or extolling (Luke 2:14) what is already a reality,"[29] explains Kittel, dovetailing the twin meanings of God's glory to his glorification. Glorifying God means affirming both what God is (his essential glory) and how God has revealed himself (his self-revelations). It means saying "Yes" to all that God has revealed about himself, in particular, to affirm what God says he has done for mankind. Call this acknowledging or extolling *glorification*, or call it by its other name, worship.

Notice how the angel in John's Revelation equates the act of affirming God's glory with worship: "Fear God and *give him glory*, because the hour of his judgment has come. *Worship him* who made the heavens, the earth, the sea and the springs of water" (Revelation 14:7). To glorify God means to worship him. "The glorification of the Triune God . . . is recognized as the ultimate meaning of worship," writes Peter Brunner in his monumental *Worship in the Name of Jesus*.[30]

The Glorification of God by All Created Things

To think of God's glorification as chiefly a human enterprise comes easy for me. As a parish pastor my whole experience revolves around orchestrating the glorification of

God in a human setting— writing sermons, conducting services, and leading God's people in worship. But I for one have some difficulty in grasping experientially the fact that others beside my kind also work the glorification of God. I do believe that God's glorification embraces a cosmological worship—a worship by mankind and also, as Brunner points out, the "worship of the celestial hosts and also with that of the non human, earthly creatures."[31] Because God made all things for his glory, he wills that he be glorified by all. Let's examine what that means.

Nature

God created the animate and the inanimate for his glory. As these created things carry out their assigned tasks, their scientific properties glorify God by testifying to his power and wisdom. Thus the psalmist writes, "The heavens declare the glory of God; the skies proclaim the work of his hands" (Psalm 19:1). While nature "has been groaning as in the pains of childbirth" (Romans 8:22) because of the effects of sin, nonetheless sin has left unchanged nature's purpose of glorifying God and her ability to do so. Paul incorporated this message to the people of Lystra (Acts 14:17) and to the congregation at Rome (Romans 1:20). Interestingly, nature has no choice in the matter.

Angels

"The angels are, above all other creatures, the agents for God's glorification,"[32] writes Brunner. In Psalm 29 David calls upon the angels to perform this work of glorification: "Ascribe to the LORD, O mighty ones, ascribe to the LORD glory and strength. Ascribe to the LORD the glory due his name; worship the LORD in the splendor of his holiness" (Psalm 29:1,2). If you read all of Psalm 29, I hope you will be struck, as I was, how the worship of God plays itself out between two worlds, the one of spirits and the other of nature. David's pen describes how the thunderstorm sang; with bolt and blast it affirmed God's presence and power. This inspired David to call upon the angels to second the message put forth by the forces of nature. Unheard by human ears the chant of the angels went up and achieved its goal, and God alone heard the worship; inaudible worship was sandwiched between the audible, resulting in God's glory.

Angels, who of course are exempted from experiencing God as their Savior (1 Peter 1:12), affirm their own reason for existence when they worship God as Creator. Brunner puts it this way: "The act of praising is the angel's nature and existence in one; his praise of God is nothing other than the reality of his being."[33]

Mankind

God installed mankind as the crowning touch of his creation. God is speaking of humans when he says, "I created for my glory, whom I formed and made" (Isaiah 43:7). If God created mankind for his glory, then humans fulfill their purpose for existence when they glorify God. Brunner, in a marvelous passage, says, "As God created man in his image, he created a creature in which his own reality, glory, might, and beauty are reflected within the boundaries implicit in the creatureliness of the foremost creature [man]. The special feature of this mirrored image, by which this creature is distinguished from the reflection of the divine essence in the other earthly creatures, consists in the fact that man became an 'I' through God's fatherly address. Therefore the mirroring of God's reality, glory, might, and beauty takes place in man principally through an intellectual act, in which the reality of God, reflected mutely and unconsciously, as it were, in the non human earthly creatures, is perceived, recognized, acknowledged, and returned to the Creator with thanks and adoration."[34]

Since God created the human race for his glory, you and I find ourselves fulfilled when we carry out this divinely appointed purpose for our existence. "Man's chief and highest end is, to glorify God, and fully to enjoy him forever," says the *Westminster Larger Catechism*. Luther, commenting on the creation, said that the "principal end of man's creation . . . is that he was to live with God forever . . . that he should praise God."[35]

Worshiping the Creator

Only the triune God, Father, Son, and Holy Ghost, deserves glorification since "all things were created by him and for him" (Colossians 1:16). Worship, consequently, links the creature with God the Creator. You will find a notable example of this linkage in Psalm 103:22, where the psalmist encourages worship, saying, "Praise the LORD, all his works everywhere in his dominion."

The creation themes, which dominate the art and craft of Solomon's temple, draw attention to this scriptural emphasis on worshiping God as Creator.[36] I thrill to the fact that this art originated in God's mind (1 Chronicles 28:11,12,19), and that God intended this art simply for "beauty" (2 Chronicles 3:6).

But I also thrill to the idea that—side by side in this art—the creativity of both Creator and his creatures confronted the viewer. On display were both the handiwork of the artists and also what their art called attention to—namely, God's creation. Think what this meant. Just as the gorgeous embellishments of Solomon's temple exhibited the creative skills of humans (who craft something into something), so their divinely commissioned nature-art would draw attention to the ultimate Creator (who crafts something from nothing). Good art does this sort of thing. The art of the temple magnificently conveyed the thought that God never involves himself in anything except that his glory be everything.

Human Nature Seeks Glorification

Isaiah wrote, "The carpenter measures with a line and makes an outline with a marker; he roughs it out with chisels and marks it with compasses. He shapes it in the form of man, of man in all his glory, that it may dwell in a shrine" (Isaiah 44:13). Nothing can better document how far man has fallen from grace and from the original purpose of his creation—glorifying God—than the sorry scene depicted by those words of the prophet Isaiah. Man worships his own image? Preposterous!

So low has the state of the human condition sunk that God, incredibly, must compete with mankind for his own glorification. This competition, this glorification of the human spirit, courts many names and masquerades itself in every generation. Some contemporary examples follow.

Crass Idolatry

Who makes an idol in reality worships himself. This principle holds true whether the idolater fabricates an image with his hands and tools or whether he spins out a finely woven man-made philosophy with his mind. Idolatry is self-righteous in nature; it can be defined as worship of the human spirit. Humans, with Satan's help, of course, invent the stuff. Luther—when he warned what people were actually doing when they led others away from Christ by their dreams and opinions—described this well: "They would lead us away from Scripture, obscure faith, lay and hatch their own eggs, and become our idols."[37]

Glorifying the Human Spirit

F. R. Webber, pastor and church designer of a generation ago, noted the effect some church buildings have upon people. Some church interiors breathe a spirit and theology which the humble in heart approve of. Others, however, feel threatened by the architectural spirit and theology that the tiles and the stones proclaim. Of such a church Webber says, "When we enter it, we instinctively lower our voices and remove our hats. Proud, self-satisfied people resent such things. One such person said not long ago, 'When I enter a church, I like to walk in like a man, with my head held high, and with a firm step. I detest a church whose atmosphere humbles me and makes me feel insignificant.'"[38]

I have stepped into such impressive, high-ceilinged churches myself. I have experienced the interior of the cathedral of Ulm, Germany, whose ceiling takes off and soars and soars. I felt dwarfed in that expanse of stone, and the feeling it induced within me was most certainly appropriate—I had entered a house of worship, and the environment dictated that God be accorded center stage. Just as the cathedral's medieval designer undoubtedly had planned it, I felt insignificant as the building proclaimed to me the incomparable greatness of God. I felt the might of this message, the greatness of God, applied to my senses as I stood beside a column with my mouth open, my neck craning upward. I remember studying keenly every detail of a monumental crucifix which was suspended directly overhead. I felt myself overpowered. Pride in my humanity would have been the last thing to cross my mind as I stood there, small and quiet and insignificant, in the coolness of the cathedral of Ulm.

How I felt in Ulm's cathedral I credit to the grace of God, because by nature you and I would rather take pride in ourselves at the expense of God. The natural bent of human beings is to build lofty monuments to self just as they did at Babel. Pride has thoroughly infiltrated human nature. Pride prompts man to seek to advance his own significance and to act as if he existed mainly or perhaps even solely for himself.

Let's move on to see how this glorification of the human spirit fathered and furthered some great international movements of the 20th century—movements in which man basically acts as his own god.

Humanism

Humanism, according to the "Humanist Manifesto," seeks to explain man's purpose in the universe. This philosophic system influences much of what shapes our society today. It has many friends and adherents in the fields of science, politics, education, and journalism who hold fast to its tenets and publicly proclaim its views. Humanism says, "Since God is dead, man is God; man is the sole determiner of his own values . . . man makes himself."[39] Humanism teaches that man exists to please himself in whatever expedient way he chooses. Humanism flaunts its anti-God attitude.

Communism

Communism, or what's left of it, is a decidedly anthropocentric belief system just like humanism—even if it advances its goals for human purpose somewhat differently. Communism has no room for God. Its atheistic doctrines seek to glorify the human spirit. Communism attempted to replace God with the state as the entity which "determines the value system."[40] Here, however, it failed. Witness how the peoples of former Communist lands are now opening their hearts to the gospel. Communism, by design, can only glorify man.

Liberation Theology

Victorio Araya, a Protestant apostle of liberation theology, describes the essence of this popular movement: "From its first theological formulations onward, liberation theology has explained faith in the God of the Bible as a demand for interhuman justice . . . to know God is to establish just relationships among human beings."[41]

Minimizing the cross, as this "to know God is to do justice" theology does, creates problems. When does liberation theology get around to the crucial matter of saving souls or of directing sinners, both oppressor and oppressed, to the cross? Does liberation theology take seriously man's eternal, spiritual plight? Araya says, "We must break, in practice and in theory, with all pessimism claiming to be based on a religious view of the human being, such as the pessimism so typical of the self styled anti-Pelagian anthropology of most of our Protestant theology."[42]

Liberation theology wants to dress itself in Christocentric terminology, but unfortunately so much of it comes through as anthropocentric theology. However noble his intentions, Araya glorifies the human spirit when he writes, "As believers, we must rip off our blindfolds and see how God's good news is being proclaimed today through the poor of the earth."[43]

Liberation theology rejects man's total dependence on God. Instead, it substitutes the Marxist doctrine of political revolution as the solution to mankind's basic ills.[44] It finds in Barabbas a more acceptable candidate for canonization than Simon the Zealot, Christ's disciple who gave up his revolutionary habits in order to fish for men's souls.

Black Theology

There is also a tendency in some, though not all, elements of black theology, to glorify the human spirit. James H. Evans writes in *Black Theology—A Critical Assessment and Annotated Bibliography*, "Black theology addresses the question, 'What does the gospel of Jesus Christ have to do with the struggle of black people for liberation from white people?'"[45] If Evans' assessment accurately represents black theology's understanding of the gospel—and I have no reason to doubt what he says—I would point out that this theological system confuses law and gospel and in the process also misrepresents the purpose of the cross.

Desmond Tutu similarly confuses law and gospel and misrepresents the cross when he says, "The chief work that Jesus came to perform on earth can be summed up in the word 'Reconciliation' . . . He came to restore human community and brotherhood which sin destroyed."[46] Tutu, as I suspect of other nationally known black clergymen like Jesse Jackson, preaches fruits of faith minus the honest-to-goodness Christocentric faith, which aims to save souls from hell. Am I too harsh? Can you remember any occasion when a Jesse Jackson or Desmond Tutu used the spotlight of national or international media attention to preach law and gospel as the Apostle Paul did before the assembled minds of Greece on the Areopagus (Acts 17:22-32)?

The liberation Jesus came to bring is the liberation of the soul from the slavery of sin. Any theology, black or otherwise—no matter how worthy its aims—which waters down the salvific importance of the blood atonement of Jesus Christ in favor of social justice cheats people by sidetracking them from their greatest need. People need to know the way to the mansions of heaven. Anything less than that, no matter how well intentioned, fails to glorify God (Romans 14:23).

The Gross Worship of Self

Hedonists and sociopaths (those involved in criminal behavior) make no pretense of how they answer the "who" and "what" of human identity. Hedonistic and sociopathic individuals reject moral boundaries. They both subscribe to the wild-life philosophy, "Let us eat and drink, for tomorrow we die" (1 Corinthians 15:32), which Paul condemned. Perhaps these two types of behavior best illustrate how deceitful the human spirit remains "above all things and beyond cure" (Jeremiah 17:9). In hedonistic and sociopathic man the sinful human desire to live for one's self, to glorify one's self rather than God, reaches its extreme. The bulging prison population of America illustrates the persistence of these widespread and deeply ingrained belief systems. Indulging one's lusts and passions, legally or illegally, represents the worship of the human spirit in the grossest sense.[47]

Satan Seeks Glorification

Behind all the attempts to rob God of his glory lurks Satan. He is the one who plants temptation in human hearts, making sweeping, tantalizing promises of pleasure and fulfillment under the condition, "if you worship me, it will all be yours." (Luke 4:7). We miscalculate Satan's intentions if we assume that Satan merely wants to act the role of the embittered loser. Having lost the battle to Christ in the desert and at the cross, his actions may bear a similarity to that of a retreating army which wreaks havoc out of spite, but there is more to it than that. Satan refuses to give up; his lust remains undaunted; he still covets what belongs to God. Doomed though his career of rebellion may be, he still seeks to make protégés of humans. He still seeks the glory of God for himself.

Coveting God's Glory

Paul's warning against conceit (1 Timothy 3:6) makes it clear that the devil's great sin in heaven against God was pride. The old Lutheran dogmatician Quenstedt states, "We may assume that pride was the first sin of the angels. We make this deduction . . . from his [Satan's] perpetual endeavor to transfer the glory of God to himself."[48]

The temptation of Eve demonstrates Satan's desire to make himself more than he was. Even as he desired what belonged to God, so he "undertook to instill the sin of pride in our first parents, the pride of arrogating to themselves equality with God."[49] "You will be like God" (Genesis 3:5), said Satan to Eve, himself the author and first believer of this pernicious and contagious lie.

Getting God's Glory

Many willingly transfer to Satan the glory which belongs to God, and understandably so. Satan can mimic an angel of light (2 Corinthians 11:3), work magic (2 Thessalonians 2:9), and act like a god to his believers (2 Corinthians 4:4). Using his many talents under cover of spiritual darkness, he continues to snipe at the glory of God by tempting the offspring of Adam and Eve on every level of human experience to deny God his glory.

Summary

1. God deserves to be glorified because he created all things.
2. All creatural activity exists to give God glory, that is, to affirm what God is (his essential glory) and what God has revealed himself to be (his self-revelations). This is the essence of worship.
3. God created everything for his glory, and he wills that nature, humankind, and angels worship him. God, however, finds his will challenged by some of his creatures, both humans and angels. Men worship themselves through various belief systems which glorify the human spirit, and Satan would have himself worshiped through all forms of human unbelief.

Advice

1. God as the Maker/Creator. How are you addressing this aspect of the Triune God? Study your sermons and devotional writings. Compare your recent work with material you produced in the early years of your ministry to deter-

mine your style in naming God. If you have been referring to God as Maker or Creator infrequently, have you been doing this in a conscious or thoughtless way? Do you see it as a problem? Do you see anything to be gained from naming God as "Maker" or "Creator" rather than addressing him more generically as "God?"

2. When was the last time you preached on the First Article of the Apostle's Creed?

3. Read *Art and the Bible*, two essays by Francis A. Schaeffer, published by InterVarsity Press. Schaeffer discusses the importance of creativity in the worship of God and the need for the Christian life to produce not only truth but beauty.

Endnotes

[22] Gerhard Kittel and Gerhard Friedrich, eds., *Theological Dictionary of the New Testament* (Grand Rapids: Eerdmanns Publishing Co., 1985), 178.

[23] Ibid., 178.

[24] Ibid.

[25] W. E. Vine, *Vine's Expository Dictionary of Biblical Words* (Nashville: Thomas Nelson Publishers, 1985), 267.

[26] Edward J. Young, *The Book of Isaiah*, 3 vols. (Grand Rapids: Eerdmans Publishing Co., 1965), 1:245.

[27] August Pieper, "The Glory of the Lord," *Theologische Quartalschrift* Vol. XXIX, Nos. 2-4, and Vol. XXX, Nos. 1-2 [Emphasis added]. This outstanding 88 page article, originally published in German, also appeared in an English translation in the *Wisconsin Lutheran Quarterly*, a publication of the faculty of Wisconsin Lutheran Seminary, 11831 N. Seminary Dr., Mequon, Wisconsin 53092. Contact Martin O. Westerhaus, Librarian, for copies of the English and German issues.

[28] Ibid., 2.

[29] Kittel, *Theological Dictionary of the New Testament*, 180.

[30] Peter Brunner, *Worship in the Name of Jesus* (St. Louis: Concordia Publishing House, 1968), 120.

[31] Ibid., 94.

[32] Ibid., 95.

[33] Ibid.

[34] Ibid, 36 [Emphasis added].

[35] Ewald M. Plass, *What Luther Says*, 3 vols. (St. Louis: Concordia Publishing House, 1959), 2:877.

[36] See Francis A. Schaeffer, *Art and the Bible* (Downers Grove, Illinois: InterVarsity Press, 1973), 17, for a pertinent discussion on the representational art of the Hebrews.

[37] Francis Pieper, *Christian Dogmatics*, 4 vols. (St. Louis: Concordia Publishing House, 1952), 1:74 [Emphasis added]. 52

[38] F. R. Webber, *The Small Church* (Cleveland: J. H. Hansen Publishers, 1937), 21.

[39] Carl Sommer, *Schools in Crisis* (Houston: Cahill Publishing Co., 1984), 254.

[40] Ibid., 264.

[41] Victorio Araya, *God of the Poor* (Maryknoll, New York: Orbis Books, 1987), 86.

[42] Ibid., 148.

[43] Araya, *God of the Poor*, 33.

[44] See David R. Newman, *Worship as Praise and Empowerment* (New York: The Pilgrim Press, 1988), 150, for a redefinement of the church in the 20th century.

[45] James H. Evans, *Black Theology—A Critical Assessment and Annotated Bibliography* (New York: Greenwood Press, 1987), 4.

[46] Desmond Tutu, *Hope and Suffering* (Grand Rapids: Eerdmanns Publishing Co., 1983), 166.

[47] See Wayne E. Oates, *Behind the Masks* (Philadelphia: The Westminster Press, 1987), 60-61, and William Backus, *Telling the Truth to Troubled People* (Minneapolis: Bethany House Pub., 1985), 229-230 for descriptions on the sociopathic personality and the tendency of this personality for self-worship.

[48] Pieper, *Christian Dogmatics*, 1:505.

[49] Ibid.

CHAPTER 3
GOD SAVED MANKIND FOR HIS GLORY

The Object of Salvation Is Sinful Mankind

The woman and her pastor had a long and serious discussion about the problem. She was the problem. She was a self-confessed adulteress, and she defended her sin in an incredibly bold way. She told the pastor that she was making her husband sleep on the living room sofa while she and her lover shared the bedroom and that the situation had been going on for well over a month. The pastor had difficulty keeping his astonishment to himself as she related the amazing details.

Try as he might to convict the woman of her sin, the pastor saw his every attempt stymied. Despite his protests, the woman professed herself innocent of any wrongdoing. She absolutely refused to repent. The pastor felt the situation a lost cause and got ready to leave.

Then, as he was bidding the woman good-bye, the woman suddenly burst out with a loud "Oh no!" The minister froze in his tracks, wondering what he might have said to make the woman react so strongly. His answer came as the woman bolted past him to a spot beneath the shade tree in the front of her lawn. He watched intently as the woman bent down and reached for a bird's nest which had fallen from its perch. Cradling it and its hapless contents in her hands, she wondered out loud what would become of the baby birds.

The minister could not believe his ears. Unable to suppress his feelings, his bent-up frustrations found voice, "Unbelievable! You can see that those dumb birds need saving, but you can't even recognize your own desperate situation." The woman returned his heated words with a vacant stare.

The Bible loves to point out that, as much as God cares for birds (Matthew 6:26; 10:29), he would much rather cradle poor human beings. God sees men, women, and children, needy but undeserving, as the real objects of his mercy.

But try getting this truth across to some people. Unfortunately, you and I could write several books and fill them with stories about people to whom we have proclaimed the good news of salvation in Christ, but who have rejected the message. The stories which distress me most involve people like this woman, people who recognize the needy situation of others but lack insight into their own lost condition. They fail to grasp the fact that they need to be saved.

The Nature of Mankind

I like the way C. S. Lewis presented the reality of sin, its destructive hold on people, and God's solution for that problem in his classic allegory, *The Lion, the Witch, and the*

Wardrobe. There he pictured sin's hold over humans as a type of addiction to sweets in which the addict will do almost anything to satisfy his longings. Lewis has his messianic hero, Aslan the lion, rescue a boy named Edmund, who has eaten a witch's sweets and, as a result, has fallen under her spell. The power of the enchantment has completely enslaved Edmund, and he finds himself more than willing to do the witch's bidding. Her magic turns him into a villain and blinds Edmund so that he does not see how far he has degenerated. His friends, untouched by the witch's magic, mourn his inability to help himself and to fight off the witch's evil schemes.

Lewis' storybook candy addict pictures the pathetic, needy condition of every human being in such a way that a child can easily grasp what he is driving at. Satan has cast a spell over humans which has left them proud people, people who by nature lack the goodness and personal integrity which pleases God, people who are unwilling to accept the picture which the Bible sketches of sinful mankind.

This unwillingness to accept the Biblical assessment of sin is found, as one might readily suspect, in many secular corners. But I find it particularly bothersome when I also locate it in modern theology's reluctance to warn about the extent and seriousness of sin. Today's theologians, blind to their own predicament and man's inherent evil, increasingly remind me of the woman who knelt to save the birds in her yard.[50]

The Bible, however, maintains that mankind, having inherited Adam's original sin (Romans 3:10-20), has fallen under Satan's spell and has turned into God's enemy (Romans 8:7). Francis Schaeffer calls this the "dilemma of man." Man, who was created originally in the image of God and then lost that image (Genesis 5:3), lacks the power to restore himself to a state of personal holiness wherein he can glorify God.

The Nature of God

In my late teens I used to work for a millionaire. My job was to cut the grass and, in general, to keep things neat and tidy on his vast estate. Very rarely did I see him because he was usually off on one trip or another. However, I always knew when he had returned because his butler would put out the word that he had come home. I knew what this meant. The rest of my grass-cutting colleagues and I were supposed to keep out of sight and keep our lawnmowers quiet. This wealthy man had been known to fire grounds-keepers on the spot if they riled or disturbed him.

After a couple of summers of working for the millionaire as the invisible teenager, I made a big mistake. One day I was, piloting my big, noisy, smoke polluting lawn mower around the estate. Unbeknownst to me the important man had come home. You can imagine my panic when, without warning, the millionaire emerged from his home. It was only appropriate that when I spotted him approaching, I was kneeling in a suppliant position on the lawn, trimming the stray blades of grass with my clippers. I figured my job was finished, but fortunately it didn't turn out that way this time.

But later that summer the millionaire did attempt to fire me. My offense on that occasion was running a noisy chain saw. But because he failed to get my name, and because my buddies played dumb when he called our shop to learn who I was, I managed to finish out the summer.

The next summer saw me working at a different job, and I was happy not to have to work for the millionaire. He scared me. My encounters with him taught me how wealth and power can create huge gulfs between people. The nature of his position dwarfed that of mine. My millionaire employer was powerful and important while I occupied a relatively insignificant station in life. I know I would have felt a little less frightened of him, if he would have wielded the power of his wealth in a gentler way.

56

When I think of my millionaire boss and my relationship to him, I can't help but compare that situation to the one which exists between God and us human beings. I think of the vast differences between God and us. I think of the richness and the purity and the power of God's holy and almighty position, and then I think of the poverty of my sinful state. As poor as I was when compared to my millionaire boss, I am struck by the thought that I can calculate my poverty before God as infinitely greater.

But there the comparison ends. Unlike my former boss, God uses the power of his wealth in a gracious way. What I am not, God is. And I need not fear the immeasurable gulf which separates us, for what I cannot do, God does for me; he spends his riches on me. God's nature prompts him to do what you and I could never have expected him to do, to spend his love on morally bankrupt people in a lavish and generous way. Call this God's grace. Call God's nature a gracious one, as Paul does: "For you know the grace of our Lord Jesus Christ, that though he was rich, yet for your sakes he became poor, so that you through his poverty might become rich" (2 Corinthians 8:9).

God's grace, therefore, colors what the Bible means when it says that "God is love" (1 John 4:8). I say this because people like to claim that God is a loving God, but they often fail to define his love in the context of his gracious nature, and people sometimes confuse the word "permissive" with the word "love." For example, in a bid to excuse their sins, some like to fool themselves by picturing God as someone who views sin permissively, excusing it. While the Scriptures certainly define God's nature as loving, they understand this to mean that God loves graciously, calling his love *agape*. Scripture defines God's agape as a thinking and a feeling which understands the needy condition of sinners—while still noting the fact that sinners deserve to be damned for their sins. In addition, God's agape also formulated the wisdom and the will to work out a solution for this predicament. God is love, because his gracious nature found a way to satisfy his need to punish sin while sparing humankind. His love settled on the solution of sending his Son to work out mankind's salvation.

God's Plan of Salvation

God's plan to save sinners involved him personally. It cost him his "one and only Son" (John 3:16). The method used to accomplish this rescue of mankind amounted to an exchange—an exchange in which God substituted his Son for sinners. This exchange took place first when God's Son became human and lived a righteous, perfect life "in service to God" (Hebrews 2:17), a substitutionary life in which he fulfilled "all righteousness" (Matthew 3:15) in behalf of all sinners. God's Son entered into the second half of this exchange when he sacrificed himself on the cross vicariously. There he tasted "death for everyone" (Hebrews 2:9) and made atonement for the "sins of the whole world" (1 John 2:2).

God's plan of salvation effectively gave sinners what he in his righteous will demanded from them: righteousness. On the basis of what his Son accomplished, God has declared all human beings forgiven of their sins and has invited individual sinners to accept this general announcement, and by accepting it, to make it their personal possession (Acts 16:31). Understand salvation, therefore, not as a case of God changing his mind about the problem of sin, but as a case of his solving the problem by satisfying his need for justice vicariously.

Even as this plan involved God personally, so it was also planned eternally, making the wonder of this loving exchange twofold. God personally performed this work—but only after he had planned to make this exchange before the need arose. The Maker of all anticipated man's needy condition before he had created him (Ephesians 3:11). In all of this, mankind finds itself the tender, sought-after object of God's love (Luke 19:10).

The Double Purpose of Salvation

Liberation theology claims Jesus as its own, making him the archetype of the political savior and claiming his mission was aimed at the betterment of the human race.[51] Liberation theology misdefines betterment, but I feel compelled to give a small measure of thanks to this political system masquerading as Christianity because, in a weird way, it calls attention to a facet of biblical salvation which conservative theology, I believe, understates.

How does conservative theology most often portray the salvation of the sinner? Lutheran terminology describes it as a rescue from sin, death, and devil. This is looking at salvation from the negative, as a rescue *from* something bad. You might think of this as the *negative half* of salvation.

I ask you to think also of the *positive* half of salvation. Salvation as a rescue to something good deserves equal treatment, does it not? Salvation comprises two equal actions: God rescues us *from* something (bad) and restores us *to* something (good).

Now I will take you back to liberation theology and explain why I can see some good in its terribly misdirected energies. Oddly, it is liberation theology which has popularized the restorative nature of salvation, the positive side of it in which God renews to sinners something good. Leonardo Boff describes the restorative mission of liberation theology in terms of what he understands Christ's mission to have been: "He [Christ] seeks to be the instrument of liberation from whatever so cruelly scourges . . . and of liberation life, for an open community of love, grace, and the fullness of God."[52] Boff would be convincing if he had chosen his nouns in as scripturally correct a fashion as he did his prepositions. Christ has liberated sinners from the scourge of Satan, renewing and restoring them for a new and better life with their fellow human beings in this world and for a never ending life with God in heaven.

Salvation No End in Itself

Salvation has an end: to restore to sinners the holy and happy relationship with God which Adam originally enjoyed but lost, so that sinners might still work God's glorification. The King James Version puts it nicely, "I will deliver thee, and thou shalt glorify me" (Psalm 50.15).

Humans were made to glorify God, but Adam's fall into sin destroyed that plan. By sinning he lost the *imago Dei*, his holiness and righteousness, and thereby he lost the ability and the status to accomplish his created purpose. The genealogical account of Adam's descendants in Genesis 5 leaves no doubt about this. Moses begins the account by stating that God made man "in the likeness of God" (Genesis 5:1). However, he does not go on to say the same of Adam's firstborn. Adam has sinned. No longer can it be said that his offspring are born "in the likeness of God." Rather, Moses notes tragically, "When Adam had lived 130 years, he had a son in *his own likeness, in his own image*" (Genesis 5:3). These cryptic words signal that something radically wrong has infected human nature, resulting in mankind's inability by nature to glorify God. Mankind by nature cannot "worship the LORD in the splendor of *his holiness*" (1 Chronicles 16:29) because it lacks the basic ingredient to do so, the *imago Dei*.

Salvation, however, restores to mankind what Adam lost. Salvation gives back to sinners the holy image of God. Paul alludes to this when he writes about those who "have put on the new self, which is being renewed in knowledge in the image of its Creator" (Colossians 3:10). And, he specifies this restoration all the more where he encourages others "to put on the new self, created to be like God in true righteousness and holiness" (Ephesians 4:24).

Why does God seek to restore sinners to holiness?

God does not save sinners simply because they need saving, or simply because it is God's nature to save. You might say that God had an ulterior motive in doing what he did. Now I know this sounds bad, because when we use this expression we almost always use it in a negative way. But I am using the expression here because I can't think of a more suitable way of expressing it. The point is that God had a motive which caused him to restore humans to a state of holiness. God saves sinners from their deserved punishment and restores to them the state of holiness so that they might continue the master plan of creation: his glorification. God is simply unwilling to allow the sin of his creatures to derail his objective. He saved his fallen creatures so that they might continue to worship him as designed originally. And, of course, in saving undeserving humans, God gave humans a second reason for his glorification.

God's Saving Ways Deserve Praise

Pip, the orphaned, mistreated boy who grew up to become the thankless, ungenerous, and very-much-in-debt hero of Dicken's *Great Expectations*, experienced a reformation of character when his stepfather, Joe Gargery, generously paid his creditors to keep him out of debtor's prison. How could Pip ever repay Joe the debt which he owed him, a debt transferred to a new and admittedly benevolent creditor, but a debt nevertheless? Said Pip to Joe and to his wife Biddy, "I shall never rest until I have worked for the money with which you have kept me out of prison, and have sent it to you. Don't think, dear Joe and Biddy, that if I could repay it a thousand times over, I suppose I could cancel a farthing of the debt I owe you, or that I would do so if I could."[53]

Pip was true to his word, never resting until he had re-paid Joe the debt which his life of empty luxuries had bought.

Sinners are likewise in debt, doubly so. The "wages of sin" (Romans 6:23) has created a debt which man cannot pay; God paid the debt. And now, you see, man finds himself indebted to God who paid off the former lien holder by the living and dying merits of his Son. Each individual then faces the critical question: to whom would I rather be in debt? Shall I remain a slave to sin, or shall I become God's slave?

The choice becomes simple after the law crushes the sinner's pride and when the gospel speaks relief to his conscience. "What a lovely prospect", the sinner thinks after the Holy Spirit has opened his eyes. He gladly takes God at his Word, is released from being a slave to sin (Romans 8:20), and becomes God's slave (Romans 6:23). The believer loves the idea of being indebted to God. He will pay God what, in a sense, he owes him—he lives and loves to glorify him, because he has now come to see God from two angles, as Creator and Savior.

Summary

1. When mankind fell from grace through Adam's sin and found itself powerless to reverse its condition, God acted. His action plan gave sinners what his law demanded of them, namely, righteousness. This righteousness God imputed to sinners because of the personal work of his Son, Jesus Christ, who kept the law perfectly and then died on the cross in exchange for the salvation of sinners.
2. God's action plan purposed to provide humankind with a salvation from something bad (sin) to something good (righteousness). This dual purpose of salvation can be understood as a restoration.

3. God, through the work of his Son, Jesus, restores sinners to the status of personal righteousness, so that fallen mankind might still work the plan for which it was created originally—the glorification of God. In doing so, God gives sinners two reasons for his glorification; he has made and has saved sinners.

Advice

1. Read pages 9-11 of the Introduction in *Preaching The Creative Gospel Creatively* by Francis A. Rossow, published by Concordia. Rossow recommends that pastors read belletristic literature, saying that novelists make good preachers of the law. Quoting the insights of writers like Tolstoy and Steinbeck into the inability of mankind to save itself from its sins can breathe realism and life into sermons.

2. In a future sermon, use the word "restore" exclusively to describe the purpose of Christ's work. Evaluate. Did the repeated use of the word "restore" lead you into a new awareness or appreciation of Christ's mediation? How were your listeners affected? (You'll have to make discreet inquiries)

3. Read *The Lion, the Witch, and the Wardrobe*, the first book of C.S. Lewis' Chronicles of Narnia, a contemporary gem of an allegorical treatment of sin and redemption. If you have young children, read the book in installments to them. See what they think.

4. Examine the ways you present the issues of sin and redemption in your sermons. Do you almost always use the biblically worded or denominationally, time honored formulas when you preach about sin and how God restored sinners to a status of holiness through Christ? Compile a list of allegorical illustrations from novels to spice up your preaching. Especially check the fairy tales; you'll be

surprised how many of them are based on the plot of justice and redemption.

Endnotes

[50] See Carl E. Braaten and Robert W. Jenson, eds., *Christian Dogmatics*, 2 vols. (Philadelphia: Fortress Press, 1984), 1:325; the authors reject the biblical doctrine of original sin.

[51] See Claus Bussmann, *Who Do You Say?* (Maryknoll, New York: Orbis Books, 1985), 56,57.

[52] Leonardo Boff, *Jesus Christ Liberator: A Critical Christology for Our Time* (Maryknoll, New York: Orbis Books, 1978), 61.

[53] Charles Dickens, *Great Expectations* (New York: Dodd, Mead and Co., 1985), 591,592.

CHAPTER 4
GOD IS
GLORIFIED
FOR HIS GRACE

The Grace of God's
Creating and Saving Ways

A nurse who worked with alcoholics in a Christian treatment facility told me the following story. In the course of one patient's treatment, she had witnessed her faith to him as she had done on numerous occasions with other alcoholics. "God loves you; God sent his Son to save you," she would say, and those on the receiving end of that news would either accept or reject her message. This patient did neither of the two—he protested. He demanded to know why God wanted to save him. "Because God loves you," the nurse answered. "But why should he want to love me," countered the man. The nurse stood speechless.

I'm afraid that I wasn't much help when the nurse passed that question on to me: "Why? Why should God love?"

I struggled for an answer as we sat in a crowded living room: "Oh, because he's gracious."

"Well, why is he gracious?"

"Oh, because that's his nature."

"Well, why is that his nature?"

"Oh, because that's just how God is."

I reasoned with myself in this manner while I sat in that living room, but my inability to arrive at a satisfactory answer did more than deflate my ego. The experience injected a bit of a nagging, bothersome irritation somewhere into the recesses of my brain. It has stayed there for a long time, and on occasion I still feel compelled to scratch it.

I'm still itching about this question, but I am learning to live with it and to enjoy it. I love a mystery, and God's love ranks as the most mysterious of mysteries. Look for this mystery, for example, in Psalm 115 and notice how it links God's glory to his love and faithfulness: "Not to us, O Lord, not to us but to your name be the glory, because of your love and faithfulness" (Psalm 115:1). Apply here the alcoholic's riddle: "But why should God love me and be so faithful to me?" The psalmist answers, "Our God is in heaven; he does *whatever pleases* him" (Psalm 115:3).

The psalmist leaves the answer of God's love and faithfulness shrouded in mystery, citing only the will and pleasure of God as the source of his love for unlovely people. That leads me to repeat what others have said in explanation of this mystery: neither creation nor salvation constitute necessary acts of God. Pieper says, "As God was a causa libera in the redemption through the incarnation of the Son of God, so also he was a causa libera in the creation."[54] Creation and salvation represent gracious activities by God; they came about through the gracious will of God.

But is God required to be gracious? "A necessity of grace must not be ascribed to God,"[55] Pieper maintains. God did not *have to* create or save. The human mind balks at such divine independence, yet recognize this as the nub of the doctrine. "God is the efficient Cause of our bliss. But he is without doubt a free Cause."[56]

God created man, though it was unnecessary for him to do so, and then he granted man salvation when it became "necessary," although this divine action was not necessitated by external forces on God's will. God, we must admit, does "whatever pleases him" (Psalm 115:3). How wonderful! How glorious! In the freedom of his will, God elected to create us and then to save us, loving us still more when we had turned unlovable in sin. The mystery of why God should behave in such a manner can only magnify this characteristic, which, more than any other attribute of God, shines as God's most glorious—his grace. The glory of God is his grace.

Paint God's Portrait Graciously

I am an admirer of Rembrandt van Rijn. As far as painters, etchers, and drawers go, I, as would a crowd of others, consider him the prince of artists. Rembrandt wins many admirers because of his technical expertise and his innovative, original style. But I also think he remains a favorite with each emerging generation because of the timeless, human appeal which his self-portraits evoke. Rembrandt produced dozens of self-portraits in the course of his lifetime, a significant number in his final years. That lifelong fascination with his face has given art critics a wealth of information, and it also continues to cast a spell over gallery visitors who pause to stare at his features and then, in pausing, ponder their own mortality.

The many faces of Rembrandt show the artist in the ebb and flow of good and bad fortune. These are symbolized in the colors and styles he used. In his early years Rembrandt's work was dominated by dull earth tones, browns and ochres in particular. In middle age his choice of colors warmed. And in old age his palette took on its richest and most subtle hues. The changing colors which Rembrandt used in his many self-portraits, revealed his character and moods as well as his fortunes. They were unique as was his style. There was only one Rembrandt.

So also there exists only one God. As his own self-portraits in Scripture reveal, he is unique in every way, and none of his creatures can be compared with him. God paints himself to reveal many sides of himself—his omniscience, omnipotence, and omnipresence. But preeminently his self-portraits reveal one dominant trait, his grace.

The Glory of the Lord Is His Grace

Do you know where God painted his most revealing self-portrait? You will find this piece of artwork, carried out in colors nearly too much for the naked eye to behold, hanging in the 33rd and 34th chapters of Exodus.

"Now show me your glory" (Exodus 33:18), said Moses to God. God did more than show Moses his glory. Unlike modern painters who seek to mystify art aficionados by their abstractness in order to darken interpretation, God explained the self-portrait which Moses was to see. The synonyms which God chose to explain his glory—I especially want to stress—are revealing: "And the LORD said, 'I will cause all my goodness to pass in front of you, and I will proclaim my name, the LORD, in your presence'" (Exodus 33:19).

Pieper sees the "goodness" of God as a reference to God's causa libera in saving man: "The goodness or the beauty of God is that which He proclaims regarding himself in the next two sentences and in Chapter 34:6,7. Earlier (Exodus 3:14,15) he has summed it up in the one name which he himself revealed, the name Jehovah . . . and its significance is free but never vacillating grace. He became the God of Abraham, Isaac, and Jacob out of free, entirely free choice, because it so pleased him, not because they had in any way deserved it of him." [57]

And so it happened. What Moses wanted to see, God drew in a spectacular, supernatural self-revelation. The cloud in which God manifested himself, however, becomes less important in defining what makes God glorious than the words which accompanied the sight: "Then the LORD came down in the cloud and stood there with him and proclaimed his name, the LORD. And he passed in front of Moses, proclaiming, 'The LORD, the LORD, the compassionate and gracious God, slow to anger, abounding in love and faithfulness, maintaining love to thousands, and forgiving wickedness, rebellion and sin'"(Exodus 34:5-7).

God's own self-portrait, a self-glorification, unique to all of Scripture, "pours out his grace upon us and ties it up with his name Jehovah."[58] As Pieper puts it, God's grace shines as his greatest glory; it stands as the centerpiece of all his attributes: "Only One can be truly gracious, he who alone is exalted, almighty, absolutely independent, who needs to seek no one's favor or to fear anyone else, from whom grace flows forth out of unselfishness, out of the pure goodness, love, and mercy of his heart. . . . And his compassionate grace is perfect, as infinite as his godhead or his eternity and omnipotence; it is free, it is God's nature, called forth by nothing on our part. I will be gracious to whom I will be gracious."[59] I am repeating myself, but it bears reaffirming— the glory of the Lord is his grace.

The Wealth of God's Grace

Have you noticed how great artists invite imitators? This happened to Rembrandt. His genius and popularity won him many protégés, who naturally paid a price for the privilege of receiving his artistic tutelage. Rembrandt, in turn, paid some of his students the ultimate compliment by signing his name to their paintings. Artists did things like that back then. Works of art were often produced in collaboration with master and students, the master putting the final touches on the work of his students. And, if the student work proved worthy, the master might autograph it.

God the artist has his school of imitators, too. I say this in a good sense and in connection with his self-portrait in Exodus 33 and 34, where he painted his grace with such flare. God inspired a school of men who through the ages would come to copy the theme of this grace in their portrayal of him. He moved these prophets and apostles to paint the history of Israel, the coming of the Messiah, and the birth of the New Testament church in the rich terms of his love and mercy and compassion.

The many shades of God's grace dominate all of Scripture, but nowhere do they shine more brightly than in the writings of Paul. To him belongs the honor as the "greatest artist after the style of God"; his inspired works of art glorify God for his grace in a way rivaled only by God's own self-glorification to Moses on Sinai (Exodus 34:5-7). No one in Scripture outdoes Paul in painting God's portrait in swatches of glorious grace, as it affects humans and their status before God. I think, for example, of the passage where he calls God's gracious ways with sinners "rich" (Ephesians 2:4): "And God raised us up with Christ and seated us with him in the heavenly realms in Christ Jesus, in order that in the coming ages he might show the incomparable *riches of his grace*, expressed in his kindness to us in Christ Jesus" (Ephesians 2:6,7).

Notice where you find this portrayal of God's glorious grace. It prefaces Paul's classic, definitive statement on justification. A sinner is saved by grace alone (Ephesians 2:8,9). And why? Because God finds himself so rich in grace. God saved sinners by substituting his own Son in their place because he felt himself so free to spend the riches of his "kindness." This "kindness" (Ephesians 2:7) of

God redounds "to the praise of his glorious grace" (Ephesians 1:6). Or, as Paul splashed it on a different canvas, "the grace that is reaching more and more people may cause thanksgiving to overflow to the glory of God" (2 Corinthians 4:15).

The Scripture writers, and Paul in particular, want us to worship God for the gracious way he used his almighty power, a sovereignty he employed independent of any creatural pressures placed on him and which he wields in behalf of mankind graciously. What God did, he did as the great "I am" that is, of his own initiative and free will. This involves both his creating and saving activities, making these two divine works ample reason for his redeemed creatures to glorify him: "You are worthy, our Lord and God, to receive glory and honor and power, for you created all things, and by your will they were created and have their being (Revelation 4:11) . . . Worthy is the Lamb, who was slain, to receive power and wealth and wisdom and strength and honor and glory and praise" (Revelation 5:12).

Summary

1. Why God should want to love unlovable sinners remains a question which the Bible never really answers directly. Salvation, as well as creation, constitute unnecessary acts of God. God created and saved humans purely out of his free will, a causa libera. Humans, therefore, find cause to glorify God because of the gracious way he wields his sovereignty, employed independently of creatural pressures placed on him.
2. According to his own self-glorification on Mt. Sinai, God claims that his glory is his grace. Paul, more than any other writer of the Bible, copies this self-revealed emphasis of God in his writings.

Advice

1. For an exhaustive treatment of the God's self-revelation of the glory of his grace, read August Pieper's "The Glory of the Lord," available from the Wisconsin Lutheran Seminary Library, 11831 N Seminary Dr., Mequon, Wisconsin 53092, c/o Rev. Prof. Martin O. Westerhaus, Librarian.

2. Do a word study of the term "glory" in the Old and New Testaments. See how many times the glory of God is connected to gracious acts on his part and arrive at your own conclusions.

Endnotes

[54] Pieper, *Christian Dogmatics*, 1:480.

[55] Ibid., 2:6.

[56] Ibid.

[57] Ibid., 73.

[58] Ibid., 78.

[59] Ibid., 80.

CHAPTER 5
GOD IS
GLORIFIED
BY FAITH

Only the Faithful Can Worship God

In 1972 and again in 1982 I journeyed to Europe to visit relatives in Switzerland and Germany. On both occasions I toured world famous cathedrals, churches, and castles. I never tired or wearied of seeing new wonders; only my time and money gave out. I absolutely loved the mystique and history connected with all these sights. And I was especially impressed by the charged atmospheres that I felt in so many of central Europe's houses of worship. I remember keenly my first pilgrimage to the Ulmer Minster, the huge Lutheran church in Ulm, Germany, and how I stood lost in thought before the cool blues and fiery reds of its windows. The year was 1972, but I felt myself curiously transported back to medieval times and then forward to heaven. Worship had made a time traveler out of me.

Not all of my fellow tourists, however, struck me as having the mind to share my bliss. I remember one fellow distinctly. He took offense at having to pay the nominal fee to enter the Minster—the church collected money from tourists to maintain the building's condition. He told his companion that he felt outraged at being charged admission to enter a church. Then he said snippily, "Well, this is only a museum anyway. No one comes to worship here anymore."

The man's outburst punctured my little bubble of bliss, and I reflected on what might have brought this man—and undoubtedly many of the other tourists—that day to the Ulmer Minster. They had come to see and to marvel at how medieval man had built this structure square and plumb and monumental, and how he had managed to fill it with treasures of wood and glass and metal. They appreciated fine art when they saw it, but few apparently sympathized with the spirit of worship which had financed and erected and decorated it so.

A valuable truth was brought home to me that day. Anyone can walk into a Christian church and admire its beautiful handicrafts. Something else, however, needs to be added before one can appreciate what the architecture and the contents of that church aim to further, namely, the glorification of God. Only those who possess true faith can worship, because only true faith has the power to "please God" (Hebrews 11:6). True faith conveys to sinners the essential ingredient which makes them pleasing to God: holiness.

Holy, Holy, Holy

One can understand the Reformation in some respects as a war of definitions over the term "saint." How does a sinner become a saint (from "sanctus," meaning holy), a holy person, before God? The question drove Luther to monastic orders to look for the answers offered by medieval theology.

74

The legalistic answers he found pushed him to dizzying extremes and eventually to despair.

Luther had many fellow pilgrims on his quest to acquire
personal holiness. Medieval man knew painfully well that
he lacked the holiness which would enable him to please
God. Europe's cathedrals chronicled the plight of pious
souls who sought desperately to please and worship God,
souls who wanted to "reach out for him and find him" (Acts
17:27). Auguste Rodin said, "The Gothics set stone upon
stone, ever higher, not as the giants did, to attack God, but
to reach up to him."[60]

The sum total of biblical truth says that only the holy
can find, reach, stand before, and please God by their worship. Isaiah, who "saw the Lord seated on a throne, high
and exalted" (Isaiah 6:1), experienced this firsthand: "'Woe
to me!' I cried. 'I am ruined! For I am a man of unclean lips,
and I live among a people of unclean lips, and my eyes have
seen the King, the LORD Almighty'" (Isaiah 6:5).

Contrast the excited but happy response of the angels to
Isaiah's fear filled reaction to God's holiness. They love
what the prophet instinctively feared, saying: "Holy, holy,
holy is the LORD Almighty; the whole earth is full of his
glory" (Isaiah 6:3). What God's angels owned by nature allowed them to enjoy his intrinsic glory; they retained their
original state of holiness. The seraph's sinless, holy nature
enabled them to be "engaged in the unbroken task of
chanting his praises,"[61] and what is just as important, to enjoy it. How could Isaiah make his what the angels called
theirs?

Simul Iustus et Peccator

Isaiah's experience puts the matter squarely before us:
only the holy can stand before God. The prophet's dilemma
also raises the classic question: how shall the unholy acquire
a personal status of holiness before God? Martin Luther re-

75

discovered the answer in Paul's simple directive to the Roman congregation: "The just shall live by faith" (Romans 1:17—KJ). In his tract *On the Freedom of the Christian Man*, Luther described how a believer in Christ comes to find himself justified before God and yet remains a sinner (simul iustus et peccator). Luther recognized the paradox of this doctrine, writing that sinners attain righteousness through their faith even as they also continue to sin daily.[62]

Faith, then, becomes the fundamental key to the issue of how sinful humans acquire a personal status of holiness before God. This faith revolves around the sinner's response to the gospel in which God announces that he has declared the world forgiven because of the merits of his Son, Jesus (2 Corinthians 5:19; 1 John 2:2). God invites everyone to believe this declaration of justification (Acts 16:30,31). The sinner either rejects what God declares him to have become in Christ, or he "apprehends the promise, believes the assurance God gives, and extends the hand to accept what God is offering."[63] "Whoever believes in him," says Jesus, "shall . . . have everlasting life" (John 3:16).

So do not ask people, "Are you saved?" Ask, "Do you believe you are saved?" The Bible never doubts or makes suspect God's saving intentions or results; the Bible, rather, questions the status of each individual's response to the gospel. The Bible wants to know, "Do you believe?" for only those who put their faith in Jesus actually reap the merits of his atonement. Only those with faith in God's Son gain the holiness which counts before God. "Fundamentally," writes Frederick Bruner in *A Theology of the Holy Spirit,* "holiness is the gift of faith, a gift given by God and empirical to him alone."[64]

Holy Worship

Would you like a question to pose to your parishioners, one guaranteed to provoke some impassioned and perhaps even terribly wrong ideas? Ask, "What is worship?"

I maintain that you could put that question to 200 worshipers, and that you'd probably receive 200 differently worded answers. And I would also assert that almost all of those 200 answers would indicate a decidedly anthropocentric outlook. I say that because I have heard so many remarks from worshipers that indicate just that—that they do, indeed, see corporate worship almost exclusively from the human side.

One worshiper, for example, told me, "I didn't get much out of that choir number." Another remarked, "Boy, the church was full. You really had a good crowd for that sermon." A third criticized the efforts of a fellow pastor as a worship leader by saying, "You talked too much about Jesus." Yes, I know, you can possibly understand these and similar sentiments in a proper way, and you and I have probably even spoken in a similar vein. Yet, when we think and talk that way, we are defining worship *as something we get out of a public service*.

But is that truly worship?

How often do we define worship *as something we give to God?* How clearly and forcefully have we made the case to the worshiper that what he does in worship he does so that God might get something out of it? I wonder—in our current drive to make the experience of corporate worship so user friendly—whether we have tilted the purpose of worship off center so that people loose sight of what they assembled themselves to do in the first place: to worship God.

Please, do not misunderstand me. I favor contemporary English and the most up-to-date methods in public worship. The church always needs to communicate in a timely way if it is to "make disciples of all nations" (Matthew 28:19) in all ages. And, I believe that worshipers should feel something when they worship; I'm the one, remember, who told you how he felt when he fell under the spell of a

Gothic house of worship. So corporate worship, in my opinion, will always retain a certain degree of anthropocentricity.

I maintain, however, that its ultimate goals will remain Christocentric. Worship, no matter how arty or artless, when produced by the Christian faithful, aims to glorify God. Call this worship a form of gratitude or call it a "Yes" to God's gracious ways, but its role is to work the glorification of God. Define public worship, or private for that matter, as a faith-wrought, human attempt to affirm that which gives weight to God's reputation, namely, his grace.

Ultimately, of course, the same must be said of all of life's purpose. The worshipful response of the Christian to the grace of God is to permeate every area of his life. Luther said that life should become a liturgy (service) of worship.[65] Faith makes it so. Faith enables the sinner to stand before God in holiness along with the angels, and faith prompts the sinner to express his feelings through the action of worship.

Faith as an Entity Glorifies God

On the way back from a football game one autumn evening, I exited the freeway and stopped at a cloverleaf to let my children get out of the station wagon and gaze at the sky. God had arranged one of those glorious evenings for all to enjoy. The northern lights were putting on a show that was stopping traffic everywhere, and we were not about to miss it either. The children and I stood on the gravel shoulder of the road, and we "oohed" and "aahed." The lights, red and green and white, shimmered and glimmered. They danced and disappeared, then reappeared from the center of the phenomenon directly overhead. Through its action and beauty the light show was pointing out to us the power and presence of its Creator.

Faith also serves to glorify God. Its very presence in a world filled with false beliefs redounds to the glory of its Creator, for faith can only exist if God so wills it.

As faith's presence testifies to its Creator, so faith also serves to glorify God through the salutary influence it wields over the sinner. By faith sinners receive Christ's righteousness, and possessing true holiness by faith, sinners then find themselves empowered to worship through the works of faith. This operative nature of faith, therefore, intends to glorify God through its salvific and sanctifying influence upon sinners. Faith achieves this goal when a sinner glorifies God for his creation and salvation.

No One Can Say that "Jesus Is Lord" . . .

Francis Schaeffer portrays the plight of unregenerate humans as a crisis. He pictures them as a hunting party trapped on the shoulder of an Alpine mountain. The Nebelmeer has descended on the group in a dense, foggy embrace. The temperature is plummeting, and all involved know that they will freeze to death by morning. Schaeffer writes, "After an hour or so, someone says to the guide: 'Suppose I dropped and hit a ledge ten feet down in the fog. What would happen then?' The guide replies that in that case he might make it till the morning and thus live. So, with absolutely no knowledge or any reason to support his action, one of the group hangs and drops into the fog."[66]

As humans we are enveloped by an inborn spiritual fog which originated with Adam's first sin against God. Because of this sin at the dawn of time, "there is no one who understands, no one who seeks God" (Romans 3:11). Man in his spiritual ignorance has had only one choice from the start— to hang and drop into the fog, hoping he will land on something. But man can be rescued from his slippery slope only when God opens his eyes to see the nature of the danger and the way of escape.

Original Sin

The doctrine of original sin, proclaimed in Scripture—
though rejected by many Protestant and Roman Catholic
theologians— continues to document itself as a fact of life
through life's outrages. The Formula of Concord calls the
damage done by Adam's sinning "unspeakable." And then it
goes on to say, "But, on the other hand, we believe, teach,
and confess that original sin is not a slight, but so deep a
corruption of human nature, that nothing healthy or uncor-
rupted has remained in man's body or soul, in his inner or
outward powers, but as the Church sings: Through Adam's
fall is all corrupt, nature and essence human. This damage is
unspeakable, and cannot be discerned by reason, but only
from God's Word."[67]

Contrary to the wishful claims of liberal theologians ga-
lore,[68] whose beliefs reject or twist the picture which the
Bible draws of man's nature, Scripture adduces no latent,
hidden spiritual powers in the natural state of fallen
mankind. Adam's fall into sin turned human nature spiritually blind (1 Corinthians 2:14), antagonistic toward God
(Genesis 8:21; Romans 8:7), and morally dead (Ephesians
2:5). Consequently the so-called free will and cooperation
of a sinner in his regeneration is but a fiction. A sinner can
no more will himself to life spiritually than can a corpse re-
suscitate itself. God alone owns the power to bring the dead
to life, the spiritual as well as the physical dead.

To show how far man has plunged into the depths of the
fog of unbelief and to demonstrate the impossibility of a
self-resurrection of man's spiritual powers, Paul describes
the gospel as a matter of "foolishness to those who are per-
ishing" (1 Corinthians 1:18). Paul then goes on to explain
why the natural man has only contempt for God's good
news in Christ Jesus, saying, "The man without the Spirit
does not accept the things that come from the Spirit of
God, for they are foolishness to him, and he cannot under-

stand them, because they are spiritually discerned" (1 Corinthians 2:14).

Completely Helpless

I think I can safely say that you would consider a person terribly wrongheaded who suffers from a problem, but who, when given the solution to his trouble, rejects the advice. I will illustrate this by recasting Schaeffer's analogy of the trapped climber.

First here is Schaefer's happy ending to the story of the trapped climbers in which he explains how true faith builds itself upon the claims of God's Word: "Suppose, however, after we have worked out on the shoulder in the midst of the fog and the growing ice on the rock, we had stopped, and we heard a voice which said: 'You cannot see me, but I know exactly where you are from your voices. I am on another ridge. I have lived in these mountains, man and boy, for over sixty years, and I know every foot of them. I assure you that ten feet below you is a ledge. If you hang and drop, you can make it through the night, and I will get you in the morning.'"[69] Schaeffer proceeds to say that, if he became convinced by the mountaineer's claims, he would hang and drop.

But, for the sake of argument, what if that trapped climber reacted in exactly the opposite way? Consider the tragic nature of such a "decision" if he responded to the voice by saying, "Nonsense. I don't believe you. I'm staying put."

Such a foolish response illustrates the nature of man's inborn attitude toward the good news of Christ, which appears to him in his spiritual fog as just so much nonsense. The Bible sees the tragedy of man's dilemma in a double sense: man by nature lacks the skills to find his way off the ledge, and when given correct instructions on how to get off, he rejects them.

81

Man can only recognize the wisdom of the instructions which originate from outside his natural thought—continuing the allegory from above—when something happens to change his thinking about what he considers foolishness. God authors this happening.

. . . "Except by the Holy Spirit"

Only God can make something happen to change natural man's perception of his gospel. Call this happening a conversion (Jeremiah 31:18; Ephesians 2:5; James 5:20), a rebirth (John 3:5; 1 Peter 1:23), or a quickening (Ephesians 2:5; Revelation 20:5), but also call it supernatural as opposed to natural. The Bible uses these terms to rule out any thinking that sinners effect their own spiritual awakening. If man opens his eyes and sees what has naturally remained hidden from his understanding, the Bible gives the credit for this happening to God. Paul writes: "We have not received the spirit of the world but the Spirit who is from God, that we may understand what God has freely given us (1 Corinthians 2:12). And Jesus said: "No one can come to me unless the Father who sent me draws him" (John 6:44), and "You did not choose me, but I chose you to go and bear fruit—fruit that will last" (John 15:16).

As Jesus spoke to dead Lazarus and commanded him to come out of the grave, and he obeyed (John 11:43,44), so Jesus can also speak similarly to spiritually dead people, "Repent, and believe the good news" (Mark 1:15). And when people obey, they obey for the same reason as formerly dead Lazarus. God in his grace so wills it.

If a sinner then takes what God freely gives him, recognizing the goodness of the news about Jesus and putting his faith in him, we will have to admit that God "grants" (Philippians 1:29) the sinner such powers. God does this through the mysterious action of his Spirit, who works on the hearts of sinners through his means of Word and Sacrament. The Lutheran Formula of Concord says, "Through the means, namely, the preaching and hearing of his word, God works, and breaks our hearts, and draws man, so that through the preaching of the law he comes to know his sins and God's wrath, and experiences in his heart true terrors, contrition, and sorrow, and through the preaching and consideration of the holy gospel concerning the gracious forgiveness of sins in Christ a spark of faith is kindled in him, which accepts the forgiveness of sins for Christ's sake, and comforts itself with the promise of the Gospel, and thus the Holy Spirit (who works all this) is sent into the heart (Galatians 4:6).[70]

The apostle Paul leaves unqualified his assertion that "no one can say, 'Jesus is Lord,' except by the Holy Spirit" (1 Corinthians 12:3). Bruner comments, "Positively, Paul sees the characteristic, perhaps the classic work of the Holy Spirit in the intelligible and simple confession that Jesus is Lord. The man who confesses 'Lord Jesus' has experienced the deep work of the Spirit. The Spirit does not exhibit himself supremely in sublimating the ego, in emptying it, removing it, overpowering it, or in ecstasy extinguishing or thrilling it, but in intelligently, intelligibly, christocentrically using it."[71]

The existence of faith then constitutes as much a matter of grace as the salvation which it appropriates. Its existence testifies to the seriousness with which God has set out to win the salvation of sinners and to bring them to the knowledge of the truth, that they might share with him eternal life and glorify him for their creation and salvation—the former insures the latter. Wunderlich says: "Like Paul, we worship God because of who he is and what he has done. But we cannot worship him at all until he first comes to us and creates faith in us."[72]

The presence of Christocentric faith, therefore, causes the faithful to work God's glorification. Its unnatural

(1 Corinthians 2:9), supernatural (Romans 8:15-17) existence points to a divine free will which graciously and lovingly crafts it by the mysterious, invisible work of Word and Sacrament.

Summary

1. Faith in Jesus alone grants sinners the status of forgiveness, because it personally appropriates the righteousness won by his living and dying merits. As a result, the worship of Christians counts before God and succeeds in glorifying him for the right reasons, for his creation and salvation. This is so, since Christian faith affirms that which gives weight to God's reputation, namely, his grace.

2. Faith redounds to the glory of God because of its supernatural nature. It too, like the salvific work of Christ, springs from the grace of God. Since original sin has rendered humankind spiritually blind and helpless to recognize Jesus as the Savior, the Christian views his faith as much a matter of grace as the salvation which it appropriates.

Advice

1. I told the story of Lazarus to one of my elderly parishioners, a man permanently confined to his sickbed. I was careful to repeat to him Christ's explanation for Lazarus' sickness, that God intended it for his glory (John 11:4). I asked this gentleman if he could see how his predicament also could possibly glorify God.

"No," he answered.

"Could it have anything to do with your faith," I asked, coaching him a bit.

"I guess so," he said, sounding unconvinced.

I asked the same question of a 98 year old woman in her wheelchair.

"Well," she told me, "I know that God is still with me. He's with me now just as he was when I was younger."

Try the question out on your people. If you keep asking your people how God is glorified in their illnesses and troubles, you will eventually accumulate a) a wealth of anecdotes for sermon material that will be attention getting and believable, and b) you will determine if you need to spend more time in your public as well as your private ministrations reminding people what a treasure they possess in their faith and what role their faith plays in glorifying God.

2. As you present the gospel, do you employ terms like choice, choose, decision, or find (making a "choice" to believe, "choosing" to believe, make a "decision" to believe, or "finding" Jesus)? What danger might you be creating if you fail to balance this out by reminding people that "no one can say 'Jesus is Lord' except by the Holy Spirit" (1 Corinthians 12:3)?

Endnotes

[60] Auguste Rodin, *Cathedrals of France*, Elisabeth Chase Geissbuhler, trans. (Boston: Beacon Press, 1965), 15.

[61] Edward J. Young, *The Book of Isaiah*, 3 vols. (Grand Rapids: Eerdmans Publishing Co., 1965), 241.

[62] Roland H. Bainton, *Here I Stand* (Nashville: Abingdon Press, 1950), 228.

[63] Plass, *What Luther Says*, 1:468.

[64] Frederick D. Bruner, *A Theology of the Holy Spirit* (Grand Rapids: Eerdmans Publishing Co., 1970), 204.

[65] See Bainton, *Here I Stand*, 231, for Luther's definition of a Christian life of service.

[66] Francis A. Schaeffer, *He Is There and He Is Not Silent* (Wheaton, Illinois: Tyndale House, 1972), 99.

[67] "Formula of Concord," *Concordia Triglotta* (St. Louis: Concordia Publishing House, 1921), 781.

[68] See Langdon Gilkey, *Message and Existence* (New York: The Seabury Press, 1979) 127-131, for a survey of modern theological heresies regarding this doctrine.

[69] Schaeffer, *He Is There and He Is Not Silent*, 100.

[70] *Concordia Triglotta*, 903 [Emphasis added].

[71] Bruner, *A Theology of the Holy Spirit*, 287 [Emphasis added].

[72] Robert E. Wunderlich, *Worship and the Arts* (St. Louis: Concordia Publishing House, 1960), 24.

CHAPTER 6
MANKIND EXISTS TO GLORIFY GOD

Fulfillment Is Working God's Glorification

How can I feel fulfilled in what I do? How can I find job satisfaction?

Some people have the type of attitude that keeps them happy and fulfilled no matter what they chose to do, while others sound as if they will never be satisfied until they find the absolutely perfect vocation. They leapfrog from job to job. They always seem discontented with their workplace, salary, or boss.

I want you to know that I am talking specifically about Christian people, because I see their weakness and/or abundance of faith as a contributing factor in their job attitudes. I firmly believe that poor attitudes toward work originate from a weak faith or an undeveloped conception of how one's faith relates to one's vocation.

How does faith relate to work?

Well, why did God put human beings on earth? To receive their worship. How? Through their work. When God created paradise, he put Adam and Eve in it, not to lounge about, but to work. "The LORD God took the man and put him in the Garden of Eden to work it and take care of it" (Genesis 2:15). Adam and Eve brought glory to God by their work of husbandry, offered to him in concert with their refusal to eat from the forbidden tree (Genesis 2:16,17). Obeying God's command to work the ground took on no less a form of worship for Adam and Eve than their obedience in refraining from eating the fruit of the tree of the knowledge of good and evil.

God gave these commands side by side, making the one no less important than the other. I say this because the command for Adam to keep away from the forbidden fruit often overshadows his order to work, as if, comparatively speaking, tending the garden involved an inferior form of worship. Had Adam and Eve fallen from grace because they had grown lazy and had allowed the Garden of Eden to become untidy, you and I would, of course, read the story with a different emphasis. You get the point. God desired Adam and Eve to work the garden of Eden to his glory. And they enjoyed their work, because they knew for whom they were doing it. They aimed to please God by their work. They knew they existed to worship God by their faithful labors.

Worship Is God's Plan for Humans

In his opening remarks to the Ephesians, Paul talks about God's glorification, not once, but three times. In each case Paul links the grace of God toward sinful mankind with the appropriate human response: worship. Paul points out that God elected sinners to saving faith "to the praise of his glorious grace" (Ephesians 1:6); that God saved sinners so that they "might be for the praise of his glory" (Ephesians 1:12), and that the Holy Spirit, dwelling in believers, guarantees to Christians the future life in heaven "to the praise of his glory" (Ephesians 1:14). The apostle hopes to give even the most casual reader the distinct impression that the divine plan calls upon humans to engage in this non-stop enterprise of worship. In other words, God has planned for you and me to work his worship.

That worship is God's plan for humans is most easily illustrated by two items that just about anyone could identify as involved with works of glorification—the worship service and the house of worship. To carry out such glorification in either case requires deliberate labor on the part of worshipers.

Liturgy

The word liturgy comes from the Greek leiturgia, originally a political term used to designate a "public act or duty performed by individual citizens for the benefit of the state."[73] The early church adopted the term and modified its meaning to refer to the public act of worshiping God.[74]

The concept of worship as a work performed for the benefit of God readily finds a home in our thoughts since the same idea expressed in leiturgia comes through in the use of the English term (worship) *service*. The German language expresses itself similarly, employing the word *Gottesdienst* (God's service). Worship then involves labor performed to fulfill God's desire that his creatures glorify him for his gracious ways.

And how does worship work to God's benefit? Luther has a startling answer. He contends that without the faith which produces worship God is missing something. I had never heard it put quite that way—that worship benefits God, in the sense that it completes him— until I ran across the following quote from Luther: "Faith gives the glory to God. Nothing greater can be given him. . . . Faith *completes* (consummates) the Godhead and is, so to speak, the creator of the Godhead—not, however, so far as the substance of God himself is concerned. For without faith God loses his glory, wisdom, righteousness, truthfulness, mercy, etc., in us; in short, where there is no faith, nothing is left to God of his majesty and Godhead."[75] Giving him the glory—that's what the Creator planned as the purpose of human existence. What more noble work then can man produce than the glorification of God by true faith? As exemplified in the term "worship service," you and I have a job to do—a job which begins here in this world and never ends, the job of worship.

Houses of Worships

Auguste Rodin had it half right when he said of the Gothic churches of his native France, "The heavens declare the glory of God: the Cathedrals join to that glory of man [sic]."[76] I like to think of the cathedrals of Europe, like all Christian architecture, as an example of work in a double sense: works of muscle and brain, and works of faith. Men built them, not as monuments to their own ingenuity, but as a witness to what God had done for sinners. In his critique of Gothic art Henry Osborn Taylor puts it accurately: "These Christian masterpieces, the statuary and facades of the cathedrals in Rheims and Chartes, do not seek to set forth mortal man in his natural strength and beauty and completeness. Rather, they seek to show the working of the human spirit held within the power and grace of God . . . . Theirs is not the strength and beauty of the flesh, or the excellence of the unconquerable mind of man; but in them man's mind and spirit are palpably the devout creatures of God's omnipotence, obedient to his will, sustained and redeemed by his power and grace."[77]

The cathedrals of Europe scrape at the heavens with their spires and tell us that the glorification of God deserves man's greatest energies and treasures. The ability of these buildings to inspire us and to fill us with awe continues to document the fact that when the glorification of God becomes the highest human ambition, there you will find man at his best. There you will find people who build their cathedrals of faith in concert with their daily vocations and who feel a measure of fulfillment in bringing a piece of themselves to God, namely, their faith-wrought works.

Satisfaction Is Fulfilling God's Plan of Worship

The book of Ecclesiastes summarizes the eventual emptiness which results from a life lived, not to God, but to anthropocentric ends: "Meaningless! Meaningless!" says the Teacher. "Utterly meaningless! Everything is meaningless!" What does man gain from all his labor at which he toils under the sun" (Ecclesiastes 1:2,3)? A good question. What do I gain from all my labor and toil under the sun? It all depends, doesn't it? If I labor for myself and fail to account for the place God rightly should occupy in my labors, I would have to say that my life could be termed a "chasing after the wind" (Ecclesiastes 2:11). In other words, in the end I will have lived an empty life.

If I live my life, however, to the glory of God, what has been gained from all my labor? What have I accomplished? By living my life to the glory of God I have accomplished something irrevocable, permanent, and changeless, something eternal—I have worshiped God, and worship of God lasts forever. In short, I have succeeded in doing something that will never end.

When I, in faith, do something to the glory of God, I can feel a sense of accomplishment even if what I have done has, in itself, only temporary value and significance. For example, I may build a tree fort for my children. The lumber may rot, and the fort may eventually fall apart. In fact, the chances are that my children may wreck the fort well before it falls apart on its own. The point I am attempting to make is this: I am building that fort out of love for my children, and at the same time I am building that fort to the ultimate glory of God (1 Corinthians 10:31). The fort itself will last only so long, but my worshipful intent in erecting it will transcend the boundaries of this life and become eternally significant. My worshipful intent will journey to heaven, and God will welcome it. Therefore, I can feel a sense of accomplishment in whatever labors I choose to occupy myself with, when, in faith, I see my intent to glorify God winging its way to heaven and joining the worship of the saints and angels. I can feel that I have done something fulfilling and eternally significant because my role in life consists in glorifying God in word and deed.

The book of Revelation teaches me to see my worshipful intent in this eternal perspective. I think of the angel who came with a golden censor and stood at the great altar. He offered the prayers of the saints as incense to God: "The smoke of the incense, together with the prayers of the saints, went up before God from the angel's hand" (Revelation 8:4). I also think of the chants that went up to God and affirmed the lasting nature of worship: "Amen! Praise and glory and wisdom and thanks and honor and power and strength be to our God *for ever and ever*. Amen!" (Revelation 7:12). I think also of the words of Jesus, which say that he sees and marks eternally the worshipful intents behind works of faith. Jesus said, "Then the righteous will answer him, 'Lord, when did we see you hungry and feed you, or thirsty and give you something to drink? When did we see you a stranger and invite you in, or needing clothes and clothe you? When did we see you sick or in prison and go to visit you?' The King will reply, 'I tell you the truth, whatever you did for one of the least of these brothers of mine, *you did for me*'"(Matthew 25:37-40).

Passages like these tell us that when people glorify God, their works of worship result not only in their own personal satisfaction and fulfillment, but they also have worked a work of eternal significance. "Only one life 'twill soon be past, only what's done for Christ will last," reads an old wall plaque. Worship, be it worked in church or at home or on the job, "stays put," leaving those who offer it to the Triune God feeling fulfilled and satisfied.

Ministers Labor in the Ideal Profession

I come from a long line of pastors. Members of my family have had the privilege of serving Lutheran parishes in Germany and in this country ever since the time of the Reformation. As I grew up, I became increasingly aware of this family tradition. So it came as no surprise that when I finished parochial school at age thirteen, I was enrolled in my church's twelve-year program of pastoral training which was conducted at various boarding schools in Wisconsin.

During those twelve years I had ample time to wonder if the ministry and I were suited for each other. Periodically I was led to question whether it was I or my father the pastor who wanted the public ministry for me.

When doubts about the ministry and my place in it crowded into my mind, I, at various times, considered joining the Coast Guard, working for the railroad, or becoming a professional artist. One year, in fact, I did more than just think about it. I dropped out of the seminary. I served as a Pinkerton Guard for one night—I could shoot straight, but I couldn't stay awake. Then I finished out my sabbatical year from theological training by driving a school bus. After those experiences I knew what I wanted to do and quickly re-enrolled in the seminary. I graduated from there in 1977, and ever since I have been serving as a parish pastor. While I can't say that I have never second-guessed my career choice, I truly love what I am doing. In fact, right now I can't think of doing anything else except serving God's people in the public ministry.

For one thing, the ministry gives me a tremendous sense of fulfillment, because I'm doing what my family had always hoped I would do. Also I'm putting into practice the things which my professors spent years drilling into my head. That gives me, as it probably would anyone, a certain sense of satisfaction. I am filling a role for which others have groomed me.

But I find an even greater, far deeper satisfaction in belonging to a profession that allows me to do something which I know fulfills my role as a human being under God in a way that few other professions can do—at least outwardly. A lot of people have trouble finding a connection between their jobs and God. I do not have this problem, for my purpose in life and my occupation dovetail and give me a tailor-made feeling of personal and professional fulfillment.

God created and saved me for his glory. Where could I find a better opportunity to spend my time glorifying him for this than in the profession I currently enjoy? My vocation ties me to the mission of sharing the gospel with others, that they too may believe and glorify the God who graciously created and saved them. Consequently, I have the satisfaction of laboring in a "job" where I and everyone else can clearly see how my vocational labors enjoy eternal significance. I have it made when it comes to finding personal and professional fulfillment; I have a call to glorify God publicly.

The Advantage of the Ministry Versus Other Vocations

In the 14th century a lay brother and goldsmith, Hughes de Doignies, caught the intimate connection between work and worship of God. He left us this record of his work ethic: "*Ore canunt alii Christum; canit arte fabrili Hugo* (Others sing about Christ with the mouth; Hugo sings with the art of craft)."[78] Two centuries later Luther, speaking to the people of his parish, reaffirmed the importance of "common" labor, stating that such labor orchestrated the worship of God, *"Denn wo ein rechter Gehorsam gegen Gott ist im Glauben, da ist alles, was der Beruf erfordert, ein heiliger und Gott angenehmer Gottesdienst* (For where there is a true obedience toward God in faith, everything which the vocation necessitates is a holy and God-pleasing service to God)."[79]

I proclaim this truth to my people repeatedly, and I have every reason to believe that you do, too. We ministers preach it, as we must, because experience has taught us that this doctrine remains a difficult one to grasp, for it challenges people to see beyond the mundane and earthly and to view their work and service from a heavenly perspective. The physician treating a patient, the clerk settling with a customer, the policeman collaring a ruffian, the carpenter driving home a nail—the earthbound nature of these "secular" jobs automatically makes them seem remote from a glorification of God. If they will become glorifications, you see, then this must come about in a deliberate way. Faith must make it so.

On the other hand, when the pastor baptizes an infant or preaches a sermon or calls on a sick parishioner—who in the world cannot see that the pastor has the one profession in life which enjoys the single-track purpose of doing something, visibly and directly, to the glory of God?

The Glorious Work of the Ministry

You and I are envied by others for the way we can train the cross hairs of our profession on the glorification of God every day and in every way. By the very nature of our profession we ministers share in the apostolic claim that God "has committed to us the message of reconciliation" (2 Corinthians 5:19), and that we are "Christ's ambassadors, as

95

though God were making his appeal through us" (2 Corinthians 5:20). We work to preach the gospel of Jesus to the salvation of souls and thus to glorify God's name and reputation, not indirectly, but directly. This is thrilling stuff! What a privilege we enjoy! What opportunities we own!

Limitless Opportunities

You and I have limitless opportunities to glorify God. I am, of course, referring to the many ministerial majors and minors that make up our pastoral duties. So I see the generalist nature of our profession as a plus—despite those who view pastors as hopelessly outdated in this age of specialization. (You may be amused, for example, to hear that Newsweek magazine says, "Clergy are the only white-collar professionals who still make house calls.")[80]

Okay, so you and I are dinosaurs. I do not mind the caricature at all. I like my old-fashioned job with its two-thousand-year-old qualifications (2 Timothy 4:2; Titus 1:2-9), and I love the endless variety of my pastoral duties. How much variety is there? In *Growth in Ministry* Marvin Johnson cites an impressive report, gleaned from a study of six major Protestant denominations, in which he lists thirty pastoral activities. According to Johnson's survey a pastor:

1. Maps out objectives and plans the overall church strategy and program.
2. Teaches and works directly with children.
3. Leads public worship.
4. Ministers to the sick, dying, and bereaved.
5. Counsels with people facing the major decisions of life—marriage, vocation.
6. Fosters fellowship at church gatherings.
7. Teaches and works directly with young people.
8. Talks with individuals about their spiritual development.

9. Visits new residents and recruits new members.
10. Supplies ideas for new activities and projects.
11. Works with congregational boards and committees.
12. Recruits, trains, and assists lay leaders and teachers.
13. Manages the church office—records, correspondence, information center.
14. Preaches sermons.
15. Follows a definite schedule of reading and study.
16. Promotes and creates enthusiasm for church activities.
17. Maintains a disciplined life of prayer and personal devotion.
18. Cooperates with social, legal, medical, and educational workers.
19. Helps manage church finances.
20. Administers baptism and communion; conducts weddings and sacred rites.
21. Participates in denominational activities.
22. Teaches and works directly with adults.
23. Counsels with people about their moral and personal problems.
24. Cultivates his or her home and personal life.
25. Participates in community projects and organizations.
26. Mixes socially to develop contacts.
27. Maintains harmony, handles troublemakers, averts or resolves problems.
28. Assists victims of social neglect or injustice.
29. Speaks to community and civic groups.
30. Visits regularly in the homes of the congregation.[81]

I referred to this list in a sermon I preached at the installation of a friend of mine. I was attempting to hammer home how wonderfully varied the duties of the parish ministry are. I did not read all thirty duties, but I did mention how many there were. Then I made a mistake. I told the assembled group, which also numbered about twenty other ministers, that I had personally performed twenty-nine of these duties. You guessed it. After the service that thirtieth item became the hot topic of speculation among the brethren. Never mind what I had said about the glories and the wonders of the ministry. They only wanted to know what the one duty was that I had failed to perform?

Have you left undone any of these thirty duties? A menu of responsibilities crowds my daily pastoral agenda—as I am sure it does yours. Checking Marvin Johnson's list of pastoral duties may reveal that you may have even more responsibilities than thirty; perhaps you can isolate as many as thirty-five or forty distinct duties.

This multiplicity of tasks gives you and me more than enough to do. Yet I believe their very number works in our favor, for every facet of the Christian ministry freely and openly connects us to the glorious grace of God, and thereby to the great theme of life—"whatever you do, do it to the glory of God" (1 Corinthians 10:31).

We ministers have golden opportunities to live fulfilled and happy lives; people actually pay us a salary to work God's glorification! Not everyone enjoys this privilege, but you and I have been called to it. Let's open our eyes wide and, like bug-eyed kids inspecting the latest wonders at the corner store, press our noses against the windows of our framed diplomas of ordination to see with renewed eyes the possibilities for service to God and his church which our public calls have given us. And, in the process, may we feel a renewed sense of dedication and the desire to be the best we can be to the glory of God.

Summary

1. The human race exists to work the worship of God. As Adam once labored in faithful worship of God in the

Garden of Eden, so let us redeemed sinners labor at giving God his deserved glorification through our works of worship. The use of the term *worship service* implies that the role of the redeemed child of God remains essentially unchanged from that of Adam in his sinless perfection: to produce worship of God. In so doing, human beings find satisfaction by fulfilling their role under God.

2. To find ways of glorifying God through one's "secular" vocation can plague people as being something abstract and somewhat difficult to do. By contrast the parish pastor has an easy time of it. His schedule finds many responsibilities, and every facet of his ministerial duties connects him to the glorious grace of God—thereby making it easy for him to do his "whatever" (1 Corinthians 10:31) to the glory of God.

Advice

1. When do you feel the happiest in your ministry? Are there particular events or experiences which give you a feeling of satisfaction? Sit down and go over your schedule of duties, WITHOUT referring to the list you made in connection with "Advice" at the end of Chapter One. Perhaps you may want to use Marvin Johnson's list of thirty pastoral duties. Grade your duties. Give the highest grade to those duties that give you the greatest sense of happiness and fulfillment. Use the standard letter grading system (A to F). When you're finished, refer back to the page of advice at the end of Chapter One, where I asked you to grade your duties in terms of what you like best and where your greatest talents lie. Do the duties that match up with your greatest talents and "likes" also give you the greatest sense of satisfaction and happiness? Do you find any cause for alarm or satisfaction in your conclusions?

2. Once I found myself hated and persecuted for my Christian witness by an angry parishioner. The experience made me lose my confidence temporarily; I saw myself a failure. It felt good, however, to recall better days and satisfying experiences, and I regained my perspective. Since Jesus keeps a record of the works of faith which his children produce, have you ever considered keeping an unofficial list of how you glorified God through your labors? Do this for reasons purely private and inspirational in nature in anticipation of a day when you may feel like a failure.

Endnotes

[73] Luther Reed, *The Lutheran Liturgy* (Philadelphia: Fortress Press, 1947), 19.

[74] See Peter Brunner's exhaustive treatment on the etymology of leiturgia in his *Worship in the Name of Jesus*, 11-24.

[75] Plass, *What Luther Says*, 473 [Emphasis added].

[76] Auguste Rodin, *Cathedrals of Europe*, 15.

[77] Henry Osborn Taylor, *The Medieval Mind*, 2 vols. (London: Macmillan and Co., 1911), 2:85 [Emphasis added].

[78] William Anderson, *The Rise of the Gothic* (Salem, New Hampshire: Salem House, 1985), 23.

[79] *Dr. Martin Luther's Saemmtliche Schriften*, 24 vols. (St. Louis: Concordia Publishing House, 1880), 1:1164 [Translation by author].

[80] Renneth L. Woodward and Patricia King, "When a Pastor Turns Seducer," *Newsweek*, 28 August 1989, 49.

[81] Thomas E. Kadel, ed., *Growth in Ministry* (Philadelphia: Fortress Press, 1980), 13,14.

PART TWO

A

PRACTICAL

THEOLOGY

FOR

SOLI DEO

GLORIA

CHAPTER 7
THOSE
FRUSTRATING
PARISHIONERS

The Object of the Changing Ministry Remains People

When my father graduated from the seminary in 1943, one of his professors gave him this advice: "When you get to your church, you'll want to establish a regular schedule. Reserve the mornings for study, visit your members in the afternoon, and keep your evenings free for family time."

I would like to hear what kind of advice my father's professor—had he lived to see the closing years of the 20th century—might have offered to the graduates of today's seminaries. You and I can still study in the mornings, but try finding most of one's parishioners at home in the afternoons. I sometimes have difficulty locating some of my "shut-ins." And family time in the evenings? Good luck. I

103

can count Fridays as the only weekday night free of the obligatory meetings, counseling sessions, or classes. Yes, things have changed!

The ministry can claim no immunity from "the ever-whirling wheels of change, the which all mortal things doth sway," as Edmund Spenser (1553-1599) put it. Change has spun today's ministry into a shape remarkably different from that which my father was ordained into back in 1943. But then the ministry, as it functioned in 1943, had also undergone considerable shifts and turns from how it was practiced in 1843.

I wish to qualify, however, the nature of the changes of which I speak. When I say that the ministry today has changed from what it was in my father's day, I am referring, for the most part, to changes in inessential things and changes in external matters.

Changes in technology, for example, have brought about radical breakthroughs in communication, and I have forced myself to adapt to them. Let me illustrate. I wrote this book with the aid of a computer. This in itself came as a big change for me. Like my father before me, whose career stretched from the era of the vacuum tube to the day of the lap-top computer, I began my career with a manual type-writer. My dad stubbornly kept to his World War II technology, but I surrendered to the silicon chip in 1987. This breakthrough has changed my study habits and allowed me to save many hours. Those hours I saved in the writing process have been transferred to other parish concerns.

You and I recognize that the ministry has also undergone transformations in respect to means and methods. In 1943, for example, no one was promoting Church Growth methods by name nor using evangelism techniques like those popularized by James Kennedy of Coral Ridge Ministries fame or employing technological methods such as televised worship services.

Even the language of the worship service speaks a different tongue. You will hear Spanish spoken today in once staunch, old-world Lutheran parishes, where 50 years ago preachers with throat clearing, guttural accents reached out to immigrants and their descendants with Luther's *Muttersprache*. And who would have ever imagined in 1943 that a half century later denominational hymnal committees would battle over gender tags in naming God and debate the merits of addressing God as "Thee" or "you?" The last half century has witnessed a great evolution in the ministry's use of methods, means, and technology.

But has the ministry changed in essence? Absolutely not. The ministry, however congregations see fit to structure it, continues to apply its methods, means, and technology to people. People remain the unchanging object of the ministry, and the underlying purpose of the ministry remains to save and serve people.

How the ministry reaches people with the gospel may well differ from one era to another. The ministry—if it aims to minister to people where it finds them—will have to adapt to individual needs and individual situations. It will have to examine its strategies, methods, and techniques continually, and it will have to retune them or discard them or create new ones to meet the needs of a changing society. I see the proper balance between the changing externals of the ministry and its changeless mission to people stressed in Paul's classic, evangelical attitude, "I have become *all things* to all men so that by *all possible means* I might save some" (1 Corinthians 9:22). Change the means, change the methods, change the technology, but never change the ministry's purpose—saving and serving people.

Working with People by Working Alongside Them

My first real job saw me behind the ticket counter of the Greyhound bus terminal in Racine, Wisconsin. I was 17

105

years old, and I worked there for the first 2 months in the summer of 1967. I made $1.10 an hour, minimum wage at the time, but I thought the wage excellent for what I did—I routed people along their journeys and sold them their tickets. After 2 months of that, a family friend got me a job cutting grass and tending the grounds for a millionaire, a story I have already related to you. Summer jobs in later years found me painting homes, painting signs, and counting nuts and bolts as an inventory analyst in a factory.

When I enrolled in the seminary in the fall of 1972, I found part-time employment once again as a house painter and then as a school maintenance man. Dropping out of school for a year, I worked one night as a security guard for Pinkertons, quit, and then drove a school bus. In my final year of the seminary, I capped off my career of part-time jobs as a janitor in a Jewish synagogue.

From ticket clerk in 1967 to synagogue sweeper in 1977, I experienced a true variety of work. My various jobs put me in contact with a colorful cast of fellow workers and bosses. In all these jobs I worked *with people*. My work paired me with other people to provide services and products such as tickets, immaculate lawns, inventory lists, well-ordered classrooms, and freshly painted houses and signs. Never, though, in any of my part-time employment experiences can I remember attempting to change anyone's behavior for the better or to alter anyone's ethics or beliefs in the course of my duties. That was not part of my job.

The objective of my work experiences from 1967 to 1977 mirrors that of most laborers. Like most people, I was involved with others in a combined effort where we attempted to match our time and talents for the production of things. The ministry, however, takes this principle one step further. The ministry aims to serve people by changing them. It matches the time and talents of ministers with that of their parishioners. Its aim is to produce new behavior, to produce lives which have been changed for the better and to the glory of God. This objective, consequently, sets this vocation, the ministry, apart from all others, even from those that are somewhat similar, inasmuch as they also aim at behavior modification.

The Ministry's Work Deals with the Whole Man

As pastors, you and I aim to change and modify human behavior; so do judges, psychiatrists, counselors, police officers, teachers, and a host of related secular professions.

But, I would also quickly make a distinction between these professions and ours. While these secular professions seek to modify human behavior—and meet with varying degrees of success in doing so—you and I recognize the incomplete nature of their tools and of their inability to deal with the problem of human evil and the deceitfulness of the human heart.

Secular vocations, interested in the problems of mankind and hoping to solve them, are limited in their ability to change human behavior for the better. They can "improve" human behavior outwardly and even inwardly in respect to mental or psychological aspects. They can, for example, make a sad person happy or a mixed-up person functional, and they can put away an anti-social individual. But these vocations cannot get at the deepest and most elusive of all human departments, the soul, and better it. They are blocked from modifying the spirituality of humans because of the limitations of the law—as it exists naturally in their disciplines and in their clients.

The ministry, on the other hand, exists to serve the whole of man, body and soul, since it alone enjoys the exclusive rights of both law and gospel. Only the ministry, in other words, can show and tell a human how to behave better (the law) and can supply the correct motive and power for doing so (the gospel). God has given our vocation, through the agency of the church, the exclusive use of the means of grace, the Word and Sacrament, wherein human sin is confronted and forgiven (1 Corinthians 4:11; 1 Thessalonians 2:4), and empowered for the betterment of all, as Paul declares, "For we are God's workmanship, created in Christ Jesus to do good works" (Ephesians 2:10).

You and I belong then to the one profession which has been entrusted with and equipped for serving the whole man in his body, soul, and spirit. Using the means of grace, we aim to take sinners and turn them into saints. By the Spirit's power we work to produce faithful people to the glory of God.

Parishioners Make the Ministry a Tiring Business

I know how to wear myself out with physical labor. For the past 10 years I have been constructing a vacation home in the wilds of northern Wisconsin. From its footings to its roof, the house represents my ability to push, pull, dig, hammer, trowel, grunt, and sweat. I have ended many a day on my building project spent, my muscles hurting, my back protesting. But though my very bones have ached as a result of my physical labors, I have never once entertained the thought of giving up and quitting my amateur building project. To the contrary, working with my hands relaxes me and gives me a feeling of accomplishment.

In fact, I even find manual labor a relief and a diversion from the rigors of the ministry. It's the ministry which I have found at times to be a very tiring business. Periodically, while laboring in the vineyards of the Lord, I have felt as if a valve popped off and let all my enthusiasm escape with a whoosh. How so? Working with people makes it so. Working with people can make it happen.

Let me illustrate. I remember one summer afternoon in 1984 when I was working in my garage on a woodworking project for my vacation house. There I stood ankle deep in wood shavings, relaxed and enjoying my labors, when a car drove up my driveway. From it emerged one of my parishioners, a man with whom I was on very friendly terms and whom I shall call Tom.

I forget the reason why Tom came, but I remember clearly how our conversation turned and twisted and finally came to rest on what I was doing. I told him how happy I was to work with my hands and how it relaxed me and gave me a feeling of accomplishment. Then I mentioned that working with people often made me feel just the opposite.

When a frown appeared on Tom's face, I immediately knew I had said the wrong thing. He proceeded to school me on how much happier and how much more satisfied I should be feeling, doing the work that he was paying me as his pastor to do. Tom had once entertained ideas of entering the ministry himself, and by his own admission he envied my full-time opportunities to study the Word and apply it. So he looked with idyllic eyes on what I did, and he had no practical way of looking behind the image he had built of the ministry to know how tiring it can sometimes get to be working with people. Tom failed to understand that standing in a pulpit and preaching does not wear ministers out. It's what happens between sermons—the during the week, behind the public scenes, one-on-one, grinding confrontations with people. This he never saw, or perhaps, was unable to see.

Yet, before I conclude this story, I want to assure you that Tom, his idealism aside, spoke the truth about the ministry. The ministry should give us the greatest sense of satisfaction. I must confess that I didn't always see this, and I didn't always have this sense of satisfaction. But the older I grow and the more experienced I become, the more I see the truth and value of this. I have slowly changed my attitude, and today I derive more and more satisfaction from my pastoral work. That change did not happen over night, but I am living proof that a pastor can change his attitude for the better. It involves, among other things, developing a greater love for people—the people who remain our business.

The Minister Works in the Heart Land

Our calls as pastors direct us to shepherd our flocks, our people. Parish work is people work, first and last. But even as shepherds often find their sheep difficult creatures to deal with, so ministers can become fatigued as, day after day, they care for their people, people who often insist on pursuing their own stubborn and wayward ways. Yes, dealing with sinful human hearts and the multiplicity of evils involved therein can often wear ministers out.

It's precisely this situation that becomes fatiguing for a minister to deal with—dealing with the wide variety of people within his parish whose idiosyncratic sins demand his attention. The bigger the parish, the wider the array of personality types you will find; naturally their accompanying, characteristic sins tag along.

How would you categorize the various personalities in your congregation? James W. Kennedy, a New York City minister, divided his flock into the following categories: the true friends and followers, the friends and followers of a former minister, the chronic complainers, the neurotics and the queer, the troublemakers, the hard workers, the leaners, the learners, the devoted Christians, the nominal Christians, the doubters, the zealots, the aged and the lonely, the sick, the meddlers, the gross and perpetual sinners, and the no-shows.[82] Whom did Kennedy leave out?

While I sometimes find it difficult and wearing dealing with so many different types of personalities and attempting to address their individual needs, the experiences which have left me most bruised and battered in mind and spirit have occurred when I have had to confront parishioners with their sins. Resistance and rejection have come my way when I addressed people's sins with a "Thus saith the Lord, 'Repent ye.'" In fact, as a result of confronting individuals with God's will, I have been, at various times, either misjudged, misunderstood, or criticized by people. Indeed, any pastor who attempts to please God will sooner or later feel the frustration of dealing with "stiff-necked people, with uncircumcised hearts and ears" (Acts 7:51). We pastors find the sinful heart a hard nut to crack and the efforts we make to crack it draining.

Raw Human Emotions

Always expect to encounter raw human emotions in your pastoral labors. You can't work with human beings in their most sensitive area, the soul, and then expect that you can escape, at the very least, occasional outbursts of human emotions. I mean this in a twofold sense. You will also find your own feelings and emotions twisted and convoluted even as you encounter the raw emotions of those you are attempting to help.

I remember an occasion early on in my ministry when a parishioner sent me a very nasty letter that caught me completely off guard. When I opened the letter, the contents, as it were, leaped out at me, telling me that I was self-righteous, negative, unchristian, judgmental, and egotistical. My crime? I had told this parishioner that she was no Christian because of her belief in reincarnation. It took me some time to get over the feeling of being persecuted simply for having passed on God's judgment. Now I can look back on that experience with a sense of humor, but at the time the words stung and my spirits flagged.

You and I will reap, through wise and unwise words and actions, a steady harvest of emotional upheavals. They come, inescapable and legion, because we are working with people, not cattle. What are we to do? I am reminded of how Luther responded when one of his colleagues quit the ranks of the clergy to take up residence on a farm outside of Wittenberg. Luther, himself no stranger to the frustrations of working with people, remarked, "What would I not give to get away from a cantankerous congregation and look into the friendly eyes of animals."[83]

How do we handle the frustrations of working with "cantankerous" sheep? Competency in ministry (as I defined it in the first part of this book) means working like a shepherd. A shepherd recognizes that his sheep need help. Similarly, you and I were called to shepherd our people because they need help, because they are troubled. The frustrations, then, that result from dealing with these troubled sheep should only underscore the need to help them and to serve them, not reject them. We, as shepherds, are to view the sheep graciously and to treat them graciously. We, as undershepherds of the Chief Shepherd, are to serve with the same sort of humility he did. We are to model our Good Shepherd's behavior, for though he grew terribly frustrated over the sins of his people and grieved over them (Matthew 23:37), his shepherdly and gracious heart refused to abandon them.

As I develop these angles of ministerial competency in the next major section, I hope to dispel the notion that ministers who are frustrated in their work with people have no other recourse to handle these feelings than to resign themselves to a dairy farm.

The Ministry Is a Gracious Business

The more you view all things from the perspective of grace, the happier you will be when you feel the frustration of dealing with sinful people gnawing away at you. Cultivating an attitude of grace remains the best way to overcome those feelings of frustration.

To discover why this should be, recall the reason for God's glorification and the role you play in it, both personally and professionally. You and I exist to glorify God for his gracious ways towards us sinners. Our creation and our salvation owe their reality to God's grace. And who has a better opportunity to remind himself of God's grace than the full-time servant of God? Our personal and our professional lives crisscross in a way that makes it easy for us to glorify God—the "whatever" (1 Corinthians 10:31) of our daily activities wants to see us vocationally modeling grace.

For example, we spend hours laboring on our sermons in our studies. Then, with whatever rhetorical skill we possess, we deliver them to our fellow sinners. We proclaim to them the grace of God in Christ Jesus, that he so mercifully forgives people their sins. And what do we receive in return for this beautiful message we have passed on to our people? Sometimes we get more than we bargained for. After we have preached our sermons about the grace of God, we go to the doors to greet the exiting parishioners. Sometimes we get complaints—spoken loudly enough for others to hear. Sometimes we receive insults—people who are upset with us sometimes make a point of doing or saying things to make their displeasure evident. And, what do we conclude from such experiences? Under the circumstances we will praise God (1 Thessalonians 5:15-18), because these situations position us to apply to ourselves the message which we attempted to pour into the hearts of our people—that God graciously forgives those who sin against him, and so should we.

The upsets which result from our dealings with God's people will convince us that God indeed must be gracious to forgive people such as these who can treat so poorly, the very ones whom they have called to minister to them! In a very real way our congregations call and support us to model for them the gracious spirit which Jesus calls his. I see our

113

work partly as a call to treat people graciously, a work that finds its satisfaction in doing what one is called to do.

A minister will, indeed, experience personal happiness as he works to the glory of God. Treat people graciously, especially the frustrating ones, and you will continue to have a desire to keep at it and not to give up when you feel discouraged. You will keep at it, because you will find your faith in Christ working wonders for you when you treat people in a way which simply does not come natural to you. You will confirm the glory of God's grace for yourself as you model his grace and as you feel it rubbing off on yourself, changing your resentful attitude towards people who have hurt or frustrated you into a forgiving one. And, you will hear to your satisfaction, both directly and indirectly from those who notice your behavior, that you are being seen as a minister, like Chaucer's parson, who practices what he preaches.

Ministers Know How to Hate Sin

To witness the evil results of sin in the lives of people and then to trace its trails of sorrow down through the generations makes me hate sin. Let me tell you the story of Jane— an alcoholic whose life resembled a runaway roller coaster. Just when I thought Jane had had enough of trouble and seemed ready to coast safely to a stop, zoom, she was off again, pitching and rolling from crisis to catastrophe. Both her mother and grandmother had been alcoholics before her. And in the course of a few years I noticed that her children were giving indications of following in the family tradition. Confronted with this tragic family history of enslavement to sin, I felt a dreadful sadness descend on me and a keen, intense hatred of the sin that had ruined their lives. The difficulty with that emotion, you will recognize, is that you always have to be careful to fight the temptation to hate the sinner, at least to be disgusted with him, as you also hate his sins.

In the case of notorious sinners, separating your hate for his sins from your feelings toward the sinner poses a tremendous challenge. I have ministered to men and women who have been guilty of such sins as robbery, rape, embezzlement, drug abuse, adultery, child molestation, and kidnapping. The older I grow, the more I understand God's hatred of sin, and the more I stand in awe of his love and mercy— that he should wish to forgive it.

Ministers Have a Choice of Reactions

Your parish and mine is honeycombed with sins and sinners that cry out for our pastoral attention. How do we handle the terrible things people do to each other, things which make us feel so disgusted? Shall we focus on the hurts, frustrations, and upsets which our peoples' spiritual problems deal us? How do we cope when, in the midst of our attempts to help them, our people turn against us and treat us as the great enemy? I submit that we have two choices. We can focus on our people and their undeserving natures; if we do, we will grow resentful as Elijah did. Or we can focus on God's grace toward undeserving people; then we will grow worshipful as the Apostle Paul did.

Elijah's response to Israel's apostasy and Jezebel's death threats was one of self-pity and anger. He had faithfully carried out his duty, but his efforts had been rewarded with an abysmal lack of support. Focusing on his people's sins, Elijah complained bitterly to God, "I have been very zealous for the LORD God Almighty. The Israelites have rejected your covenant, broken down your altars, and put your prophets to death with the sword. I am the only one left, and now they are trying to kill me too" (1 Kings 19:10). Elijah saw only how the people had rejected God and how they had rejected him.

Focusing on the sins of others creates bitterness in Christian people. I know. I once had occasion to walk in Elijah's footsteps. Just as he did, I donned a habit of self-pity and anger. I grew embittered when I found myself attacked by Sally, an outstanding member of the congregation. She was active, committed, a loyal daughter of the church—a pastor could not have desired a better parishioner.

One day, however, Sally blew up and raked me over the coals. A misunderstanding about the eligibility of her son to join the church was the spark that struck the conflict. Sally's son had once been involved in some serious trouble, but he was in the process of straightening out his life. As part of his attempt to get back on the straight and narrow, he was seeking membership in our church. When I asked questions about her son's past problems, Sally jumped to the conclusion that I was looking for the sort of information that would keep her son out of the church. Nothing could have been further from the truth. In reality, I was looking for clues in his past history that would have enabled me to help him when he joined the church. Sally's misjudgment of my intentions qualified as a classic case of how to put the worst construction on someone's actions.

Sally's misconstruing of my intentions quickly flamed into a conflagration of personal attacks against me. I found myself being criticized for being too busy, for lacking a poker face in church meetings, for playing favorites, and for being unsociable. I sat there stunned, wondering, "Where did this all come from, when all I wanted to do was to help the woman's son?"

After all of Sally's words and emotions had boiled over, I tried to explain my true intentions. Sally noted that she had apparently misread my words. But the damage was done. I had heard and witnessed what Sally probably would never have said and done under different circumstances. I had triggered this avalanche of passions simply by asking her questions about her son's misdeeds. This had hurt and embarrassed her deeply. She had reacted defensively, and I have no doubt that the passions she had unleashed against me would have found their mark on anyone who had dared to open up that closetful of trouble. Unfortunately for me, I was the one who had turned the doorknob unawares, and it had all tumbled out on me.

My pastoral relationship was never quite the same with Sally. Oh, we made up—sort of. Afterwards Sally always treated me with respect, but at the time I allowed my hurt feelings to fester and interfere in the way I thought about Sally.

I have two observations I would like to make about this incident. Sally never apologized for her outburst; she may have been embarrassed for the way she acted, but she never told me, "I'm sorry for misjudging you." And I failed to focus on her forgiveness from the very beginning. I could only think about the unfairness and injustice involved in her blow up, and when I failed to receive the apology I thought I had coming, I refused to banish my hurt feelings. I behaved as I have seen children do on countless occasions; like a little kid, I wanted to stay mad and nurse my feelings that I had been the victim of unfair play. I was determined to focus my attention on the issue of unfairness rather than on forgiveness, and I paid the price emotionally and spiritually.

So much for illustrating how to copy Elijah's spirit of self-pity and bitterness.

Now consider the radically different response of the Apostle Paul to the hurts he received from his fellow countrymen in his ministerial travels. He took a totally different tact from that of Elijah's. Reflecting on the abject spiritual condition of most of his countrymen, Paul told the Romans, "I speak the truth in Christ—I am not lying, my conscience confirms it in the Holy Spirit—I have great sorrow and unceasing anguish in my heart. For I could wish that I myself were cursed and cut off from Christ for the sake of my brothers, those of my own race, the people of Israel" (Romans 9:1-4).

When I consider how much more Paul suffered than I ever did, I am truly amazed at such an attitude. He was tormented at the hands of his fellow Jews, and still he had such a forgiving and caring heart for them. I see in Paul's attitude the key to ministerial competency which I drew attention to earlier in this chapter, that of being humble and acting like a shepherd. How could he act like this towards people who had wronged him so repeatedly? I can only explain it on the basis of his deep appreciation for grace, the likes of which he, "the worst of sinners" (1 Timothy 1:15), had experienced personally, and on the basis of his belief that God wanted everyone, including his personal enemies, to be saved (1 Timothy 2:4).

The grace of God removed the bitterness from Paul's heart. By focusing on the "glorious grace" (Ephesians 1:6) of God, Paul rose above personalities and personal frustrations to turn the world upside down for Christ (Acts 17:6).

By the grace of God I confirmed this truth to myself in my dealings with Lois, a middle-aged woman who at one time had subjected me to a regular schedule of petty and rude treatment.

Lois managed to get herself into all sorts of trouble; she was her own worst enemy. She had a reputation for telling lies and making up silly rumors about people. Because she was not a very clever liar, she often managed to trap herself in her lies. As a result, she embroiled herself in many difficulties with people. Compounding the problem was the fact that Lois refused to admit that she had a problem with lying, and her husband and children blindly sided with her. When I attempted to counsel her, Lois put the worst construction on my efforts to help, and she made it her goal to get me.

Lois did her best to snub me publicly, doing some very childish and embarrassing things in the process. She refused to shake my hand at the church doors after services. She made faces at me in public. She said nasty things to me loud enough so that other parishioners could hear.

Naturally I was upset about the way I was being treated. But I refrained from retaliating. From the start I was determined to forgive Lois. I challenged myself to fight off the self-pity which I had wallowed in earlier when Sally had blasted me. Lois was looking for a fight, but I refused to give her one. I let her insults and words go by. It was extremely difficult for me, of course, to stand at the church doors week after week, greet the worshipers, watch Lois approach, feel myself go tense, smile at Lois, say "Good morning," and refuse to pick up the gauntlet and parry with her.

I am convinced that, initially, my refusal to fight angered Lois more than anything else I could have said or done to her. I managed to find the strength to act in this unnatural way by focusing on Lois's forgiveness, not my hurt feelings. When she would fire a salvo of insults at me, I would forgive her. I prayed for her and kept on praying for her. It worked. I could not feel angry toward her while I was praying for her and asking God to forgive her. I focused on the fact that, in spite of her unloving behavior, she remained the object of God's tender love.

My experience with Lois became a turning point in my attitude towards parishioners. The truth that this is what God and his grace are all about, that he truly does love the unworthy, had finally found a home in my heart. Yes, people are undeserving; and they sometimes show this trait by treating unfairly the very ones who try so hard to shepherd their souls! Yet, that very fact should cause us all the more to retreat into the glories of God's grace, and practice it.

Lois changed her behavior when she realized that I was not about to change mine and retaliate in kind. How I treated her finally changed how she acted towards me. My prayers and my forgiving her paid off, because it was reflected in my attitude, an attitude that Lois could now read. She and I reconciled and became friends.

Peace comes to those who retreat into the riches of God's grace when they have grown frustrated with people. If you and I can learn once and for all to view the sins of our people through the lens of God's grace, it will also deepen our understanding of God's undeserved love for us. How does this attitude further ministerial competency? My answer: Who can shepherd the people of God better than those who understand and love to copy the gracious treatment of the Great Shepherd for unworthy sinners, for undeserving sheep?

Summary

1. The ministry has undergone many changes outwardly as congregations restructure means and methods and adapt to changing technologies in order to reach people where they are. While many other vocations are similar to the ministry in the respect that they attempt to modify human behavior, only the Christian ministry can serve the whole man because it addresses the needs of the soul with the Word of God.
2. Working with people in their most sensitive area, the soul, has its frustrations. The minister must often encounter raw human emotions, his own, as well as those of the people to whom he ministers. The variety of personality types and their accompanying sins that a pastor finds among his people can often wear the pastor out when he reaps their spiritual resistance or their outright hostility to God's will.
3. The best way to handle the frustration of dealing with sinful people is to forgive them and to treat them graciously. When ministers are faced with frustrating sinners, they can choose to focus on their sins and unworthiness, as Elijah did, and grow resentful, or they

can focus on their forgiveness, as Paul did, and grow worshipful.

4. Treat people graciously, and you will detect the power of God's glorious grace working in you, enabling you to keep at your work with people and to fight discouragement.

Advice

1. Take a sheet of paper. Divide the paper into three vertical columns. At the top of the left hand column, make the heading: "Parishioners who frustrate me." Head the center column with the title: "Why?" And, for the heading at the top of the right hand column, write: "Do I need to forgive them?/pray for them?" Commence filling in the columns with as many answers as you can think of.

The purpose of this project is to determine which people in your congregation frustrate you badly enough that you need to do something about the situation. I suggest that you then arrange the names of these individuals in a prioritized manner, from those who are the most frustrating to the least. When you have arrived at a clear picture of the people who head your list and the reasons they do so, then deliberately set out to treat these people in such a gracious fashion, praying for them too, that you can eventually cross them from your list or lower their priority rating. Add names to your project as needs be.

2. Working with the soul often embroils ministers in emotional upheavals. How emotionally stable and mature are you? Consider testing yourself with the "Minnesota Multiphasic Personality Inventory," a standard psychological tool which can accurately indicate emotional disturbances. It is self-administered but clinically evaluated. For information, contact Minnesota PsychTests, Inc., Roseville Professional Center, 2233 N. Hamline Ave., Suit 435, St. Paul, MN 55113.

Endnotes

[82] See James W. Kennedy, *Minister's Shop-Talk* (New York: Harper and Row Publishers, 1965), 39-48 passim.

[83] Bainton, *Here I Stand*, 260.

CHAPTER 8 UNFINISHED BUSINESS AND FAILED OBJECTIVES

Ministers Often See Few Accomplishments

I love making things with my hands—always have. Thirty years ago, my brothers and I were engaged in building our neighborhood's biggest and best model railroad. My specialty was the scenery, and our HO rolling stock chugged down from my hand-crafted hills, fields, and streams and on through the lighted streets and simulated junkyards I had created. Presently I am on my fourth railroad set (It's for my children, right?), and my basement resembles a miniature kingdom of rolling plaster hills in the thralls of an encroaching urban sprawl.

I get a special feeling when I plan something, whether I am designing a turntable to expedite my fleet of locomotives or a new banner for Easter. It's also fun to execute that plan and to be able to see the results, the completion of the plan, the goal achieved. There is a natural feeling of satisfaction I find in most physical labor, the "sweat" (Genesis 3:19) of my brow notwithstanding. Put it this way—the results of the plan, the *visible* accomplishments tell me that all my efforts have been justified.

The word *visible* is at the heart and core of the argument I am advancing. After you go to work and carry out what you have planned, you experience satisfaction. How much satisfaction you derive from your accomplishment will, of course, be determined by how closely your finished product resembles the original concept. You get the picture?

On the other hand, I am often unable to see direct and visible results from my ministerial efforts. While I have many specific objectives and plans which guide me in my parish work, determining how successful I have been in carrying out those parish strategies is, for the most part, difficult. I cannot determine the success of my ministerial work in the same way I can determine my success in building a plaster ravine for my railroad set according to a preconceived plan. Some ministerial accomplishments I can see with my eyes, but others are more elusive. The ministry works with the sinful heart, and so my eyes are often blocked from seeing what effect my labors have had in this invisible realm. It would be nice to see what my efforts have produced, but the only perfect and accurate calipers used to measure success or failure in spiritual matters are employed by God—his eyes (Psalm 11:4).

The Ministry Is Often an Invisible Work

The field where the ministry's labors take place makes documentation of success difficult. Call that field the heart or the soul of man—only God sees this area perfectly. "The LORD does not look at the things man looks at. Man looks at the outward appearance, but the LORD looks at the heart" (1 Samuel 16:7), said God to Samuel. God's vision extends to the invisible regions of faith and belief (1 Chronicles 28:9; Jeremiah 17:10; Matthew 12:25; 22:18; Mark 2:8). His eyes alone see whether or not a human being believes, and he alone knows to what degree a human being makes spiritual progress.

You and I also can judge belief and unbelief, and we can in a certain limited respect judge degrees of spirituality. But unlike God, our eyes can penetrate just so far. We see only what faith, or the lack of it, produces. We do not see the essence of spirituality, only its evidence. So wrote James: "What good is it, my brothers, if a man claims to have faith but has no deeds. Can such faith save? Suppose a brother or sister is without clothes and daily food. If one of you says to him, 'Go, I wish you well; keep warm and well fed,' but does nothing about his physical needs, what good is it? In the same way, faith by itself, if it is not accompanied by action, is dead" (James 2:14-17).

This call for sanctification from James indirectly highlights the tension which plagues ministers as they seek to determine the effectiveness and the nature of their accomplishments in respect to their parishioners. Since faith is invisible, ministers can measure their accomplishments and find satisfaction in their labors only by examining the vagaries of their people's good works. You see the problem—you do not always know how well your efforts to build up the faith of your people are faring, because appearances are so deceiving and what you hope to see achieved may be a long time in coming.

The invisible nature of much of our ministerial work fuels the temptation for us to throw ourselves into those projects which give us immediate feedback because the results of such projects (e.g., building projects) can be visibly gauged. We do this to have some measure of personal satisfaction.

I have just been through a major building project in my current parish, and it left me feeling tremendously satisfied because I got to see some visible, concrete results of my planning. In fact, I can see the results whenever I look out of my study windows, for running the entire length of my driveway stands the towering concrete wall of a newly erected multi-purpose building. And I dare say, that if someone asked me to point to an accomplishment of my ministry, I would probably wave my finger in the direction of this building.

Things like building projects excite us just because we can see some visible, tangible results. On the other hand, making a call on an aged parishioner who is languishing in bitter loneliness presents itself as a less exciting prospect simply because there are rarely any such visible, tangible results that tell us what we have accomplished in the process of such a visit. We do look on the outward appearance, and we are terribly tempted to give our attention to the types of gains and results and accomplishments our eyes can observe.

Measuring Faith by the Calipers of Works

I surveyed a select group of Milwaukee area Protestant pastors, asking them the following question: "How do you measure the success of your ministry?"

Norman Whitney, an Assembly of God minister, measures the success of his ministry by "the number of people coming to Christ and by the evidence of lives bearing Christlike character."[84]

Missouri Synod Lutheran pastor Robert Bernhardt said, "I look for evidence of spiritual growth in the words and actions of my members."[85]

John Davis, another Assembly of God minister, looks for "the changing of lives through the gospel."[86]

Bob Young, Jr., a pastor in the Evangelical Lutheran Church in America, measures success as "the extent to which 'card carrying' members work side by side with neighbors to ease misery." [87]

Kevin Froelich, also a pastor in the Lutheran Church—Missouri Synod, looks for "growth of and involvement by the people, especially regarding the Bible, and second, numerical growth of the congregation." [88]

You would expect answers such as these. I do sense however, that these pastors were searching for a reliable gauge with which to measure the fruits of faith. So just what sort of gauge or scale are you and I going to use to determine the satisfactory relationship between the amount of labor we put into our ministerial tasks and the expected results or accomplishments?

How does a minister, for example, measure the success and effectiveness of his Sunday sermons? Depending on his skills and schedule, the typical minister may spend five or ten or twenty hours during the week preparing his Sunday sermon that will take him approximately twenty minutes to deliver. He may then preach it once, or twice, or three times—in some cases more. After he has delivered it, how then does he determine whether all the labor he put into that sermon was worth it, whether it accomplished anything? Does he judge by the number of sleepers? Should he measure by the reactions he receives at the door? Should he seriously accept what his wife or children say when he prompts them at the dinner table, "How was the sermon?"

I remember how well I felt my labors went the first time I preached a sermon. It was the summer of 1973, and I was invited to preach at St. John's in Burlington, Wisconsin. I went armed with my class sermon, a long and exhaustive treatment of the wonders of heaven. That sermon represented the wealth of all the theological insights and wonders I had collected in my college days, and once I had put it to paper and committed it to memory, I figured my sermon would set the city of Burlington on fire. But right from the opening gun, an old timer, sitting practically under the shadow of the pulpit, seemed determined to sink my spirits. He pinned his head to the stony wall and made like Jacob and dreamed the minutes away while I preached. I was so mad I could have rifled my pulpit Bible at him! I had wasted my time, I figured.

The invisible nature of faith hampers an accurate measurement of spiritual results. Trying to trace fruits of faith in individual parishioners to the ministerial acts which produced them is well nigh unto impossible. While I know that I preached to hundreds of people on that Sunday in 1973, the failure of that one man to listen to what I had to say spoiled the occasion for me. Undoubtedly others listened and, perhaps, learned from what I said, but my perception of the success or failure of my efforts was determined subjectively by what I saw, and what I saw left me feeling as if I had failed.

I have also communed thousands of people since the day I was ordained into the ministry in 1977. I *believe* that much spiritual good has resulted from this work. But if you would ask me if can I identify one work of charity produced by a parishioner's communing experience, or if you would ask me if any of my parishioners have at any time informed me that partaking of Holy Communion inspired them to a specific deed of Christian love, I would have to answer, no.

Short-term Assignments Versus Long-term Accomplishments

In addition to asking pastors, who had spent years in the ministry, for their opinions about their work, I also surveyed seminary students, trying to ascertain how they viewed the vocation to which they aspired. I asked students from my alma mater, Wisconsin Lutheran Seminary, located in Mequon, Wisconsin, "What is the purpose (goal) of your future parish ministry?" 100 percent of the students polled spoke of their future ministries in terms of tasks and assignments. The following sample statements will give you some idea of how they perceived the goals of their ministry.

"The purpose of my future ministry is to harvest the fields that are ripe."[89]

"To encourage and uplift existing Christians."[90]

"To squeeze out of my life as much as I can with the gifts God has given me in serving my fellow man in two areas: discipleship and evangelism."[91]

"The two main goals in my ministry are to bring God's message of salvation to life for my people and prospects and to work with youth, showing them God is an important part of their lives."[92]

"Proclaim Christ."[93]

"To put people, both Christian and non-Christian, in contact with the Means of Grace."[94]

"The goal of my ministry is winning and keeping souls for God's kingdom."[95]

"To proclaim and defend the Word of God in its truth and purity. To instruct in a clear manner the Word of God revealed in the Bible to all who are in my care."[96]

Every respondent described the purpose of his future ministry as a task in which he would either preach, teach, lecture, harvest, nurture, encourage, uplift, disciple, evangelize, proclaim, inspire, motivate, sow, win, communicate, defend, instruct, or shepherd. I would have been disappointed to find an answer which failed to view the purpose of the ministry in terms of a particular task.[97]

I asked a similar question of ministers in the field: "What is the ultimate goal of your ministry?" These pastors told me that they worked to communicate, lead, disciple, win, preach, encourage, motivate, pray, equip, teach, administer, commune, and help.[98]

I suppose I could have polled a thousand more pastors and seminarians to make my survey "more scientific," but I feel the responses would have been almost identical to those I have already reported to you. Ministers and soon-to-be ministers see themselves as task-oriented in terms of their goals, and for the most part I identify these tasks as short-term in nature (sermons, Bible classes, meetings, counseling sessions, and visitations).

Another question emerges: How will these ministers who describe the purpose of their ministry in terms of tasks like preaching or nurturing be able to measure their long-term accomplishments? I think the answer is that there are certain factors or elements that will prevent these ministers from ever learning just how successful their efforts have been. These elements will frustrate them and keep them from drawing satisfaction from their labors. Two of these elements or inhibiting factors are space and time. To illustrate: before a minister can gauge the long-term accomplishment of a short-term task such as a building program, he may have moved to a different parish—the element of space. Or before he can determine the effectiveness of his evangelism activities, he may retire or even be called home to God—the element of time.

How many of us, for instance, have not spent time sowing the seed of the gospel and yet failed to see it sprout in the hearts and lives of those where it was cast? We may wonder what has been accomplished by our sowing because we fail to see timely results or because we move away from the field before the real harvest takes place.

I used to commune an elderly, female parishioner, Marie, in her residence. When I came to her house, Marie's husband Herb would always politely usher me to his wife's side. Then he would excuse himself. Herb did not want to be in the same room when I ministered to his wife. As I learned from my father, who had ministered to Marie for years before I did—I succeeded my father in my current parish—Herb had acted in the same fashion in my Dad's time. In fact, his history of disregard for the gospel stretched back into the days of my father's predecessor, who had ministered to Marie in the 1930s and 1940s. In short, for years Herb had seen no use for religion.

The time came when Herb became sick, sick enough to warrant hospitalization. Marie wanted to know if I would visit Herb in the hospital? She was a dear woman and wanted her husband to come to faith. Yes, I said, and I went to visit Herb, determined to witness to him.

On my first visit with Herb, I happened to break in on his lunch hour. I attempted to witness to him while he ate but that proved fruitless. The next time I saw Herb, he was in terrible shape. Advancing cancer was quickly doing its work. I went to work, proclaiming law and gospel, explaining the state of his soul and his need to repent, and the saving work of Jesus. I was amazed to hear him say he was sorry for his sins.

"Do you believe in Jesus for the remission of your sins?" I asked.

"Yes," came his feeble reply.

I assured him of his salvation, and then I asked, "Have you ever been baptized?"

"No," he answered.

"Would you like to be baptized?" I explained what it meant.

"Yes," he said, "I'd like baptism."

I took a Dixie cup, filled it with water, and baptized him.

I then went out and told his wife Marie what had happened. Strangely enough, she had been admitted to the same floor of the same hospital because of an ailment of her own. She greeted my announcement with joy and relief; she was seated in a wheelchair just outside her husband's sickroom.

Herb died eleven days after he was baptized. It happened on a Saturday morning. As I taught my catechism class that morning, I felt relieved about his eternal fate. I returned home shortly before noon to get a message that Marie had died a couple hours after being informed of Herb's death!

I was floored by this set of circumstances. I thought about the many occasions that my father, his predecessor, and Herb's family had witnessed to Herb about Jesus Christ for years, and nothing had happened. Nothing. Absolutely nothing. Or so it seemed. Then, in his dying days, along I came, practically a stranger. And I had bungled my first attempt to witness to him. But my second attempt bore fruit. Why? I think you know why.

I like to think of all my ministerial tasks in the context of Christ's parable of the sower. You and I sow the seed, and we hope it takes root. Time and space may allow us opportunities to water and cultivate, but we may never see the harvest completed. Paul's words illustrate the mystery and dynamic of broadcasting one's seeds: "I planted the seed, Apollos watered it, but God made it grow" (1 Corinthians 3:6).

Through the use of time-lapse photography you can actually watch a plant grow. But we ministers are often prevented from seeing the long-term accomplishments which sprout from our short-term assignments. I do not know how often or how many times my father witnessed to Herb, nor can I assign a number to the occasions when he heard a gospel invitation from my father's predecessor or from his own family. But I can say that the seed had been planted, and I praise God that I was put into a position where I saw it sprout and grow unto the harvest. And, that's the way it must remain for much of our work. We will enter the field of our parishes each day, reach into our bags of seed, and broadcast, knowing that another pastor may first see the harvest.

Many ministerial accomplishments, perhaps the majority, will be known only to God. We may see that our efforts were successful only in the light of eternity. But if that is the case, how then will we arrive at a reasonable degree of personal satisfaction in the performance of our work? You should see this as a critical matter of faith—your faith. I believe that our greatest sense of satisfaction arises as we see our faithful labors on behalf of our people working the immediate accomplishment of God's glorification, and that really is all that is necessary for us to know.

To Worship God
Is the Greatest Accomplishment

If you would ask any of my active parishioners, "What does your pastor enjoy most about his ministry?" I am sure that the majority would answer, "He loves conducting the worship services." And I do.

My most satisfying moments in the ministry characteristically see me planning festival liturgies, designing banners and paraments, and writing and preaching special sermons and homilies. I enjoy the exhilaration of these special times when faith is displayed and God seems so close and glorious. And, naturally, I am happy to receive appreciative comments from the worshipers.

I will have to admit, in fact, that I have far too often looked for appreciative worshipers as the basis of satisfaction for my labors. I need only to tell you what happened to me one Christmas to illustrate the danger of this tendency. One year, as I was working out my plans for the Christmas holiday, the "brilliant" thought came to me that I should center my sermon on the Nativity around the coin which Joseph probably used to pay his census tax, the silver denarius.

I called a Chicago coin dealer, and I succeeded in "renting" this Roman coin for my Christmas Day sermon. I called my sermon, "If This Coin Could Only Talk!" and I had my nine-year-old daughter walk up and down the aisles passing the coin to the worshipers so they could inspect it while I preached. And the clincher to the sermon lay in the

133

neat revelation that the Latin inscription on the coin read, "Caesar Augustus, the Son of God." You can imagine what kind of homiletical mileage I got out of that—Joseph, going to Bethlehem where the Son of God would be born, and going there with a coin in his pocket bearing a counterfeit inscription. What a tailor-made conclusion!

Well, I confess that I could hardly wait to get to the doors to catch the comments from the worshipers, once the sermon, like a steamship docking majestically at its berth after a successful voyage, came to an end. I had a winner, and I was looking for the brass band, and yes, I got the treatment. And making the day perfect, I had the satisfaction of having a seminary professor of homiletics sitting in attendance and of hearing him gush praise on my work. You can well imagine how I felt the rest of Christmas Day and the duration of the holiday season.

Two weeks after my Christmas triumph, however, I delivered an Epiphany sermon which sizzled, then fizzled, and finally snuffed itself out. A depressed preacher walked back to his parsonage after that dud, one who felt flatter than a roadside kill. Serves you right, you are thinking, and I will admit that I had set myself up for such a mighty tumble because I had put too much stock into hearing and enjoying and looking forward to the favorable comments of the worshipers.

This humbling experience taught me about the dangers which exist in eating up the praise of parishioners: you can begin to regard yourself as the object of the people's worship! Writes minister Harold Lohr, "In increasingly sophisticated ways, people are tempted to put stone upon stone, building their private altars, and then scramble up on them to await the praise that belongs to God. Human efforts and accomplishments can become diversions, turning attention from God to self."[99]

Is it possible for a minister to turn the worship of God into a "sophisticated" form of self-idolatry in the pursuit of his own satisfaction? Lohr answers, "There is nothing new in that. That is the self-satisfaction of the stereotypical Pharisee."[100]

Yes, since we occupy the public limelight, we need to sensitize ourselves to the constant danger of self-aggrandizement.

How to meet and beat this temptation once again involves the matter of faith. It involves remembering that the grand purpose of life is to glorify God through faith and by appropriate faith-filled actions and to recognize how our various parish tasks fit into this grand purpose and plan. I submit that the greatest accomplishments of our ministries happen when we orchestrate the worship of God through our private or public ministrations, and that brings me to the promise which I made previously—that the pastor who ministers soli deo gloria will experience a real sense of accomplishment.

Faithful Labors Are Satisfying

I demonstrated in Chapter 5 that we can glorify God only by faith, and that the purpose of worship is to gather the faithful and to organize their praise of God for his grace (which constitutes the reason for his glorification—cf. chapter 4). We ministers, therefore, can tell ourselves— when we have labored to promote faith in God and praise for his gracious ways in the pulpit, in the classroom, in the study, in the sickroom, and in countless other places—that we have accomplished something, something great: we have accomplished the glorification of God.

When you and I, therefore, see something like a sermon or service or building project succeed and hear the praise of parishioners, we are faced with a great challenge: to remember that ultimately we labor to glorify God. Call this the successful minister's challenge: to see his narrow anthropocentric activities always within the wider circle of

God's glorification. Failure to do so means to risk the loss of one's success.

I maintain that the properly motivated minister will find his labors satisfying even when the outward results of his tasks and duties defy human measurement. Lutheran pastor, Larry Jost, puts it beautifully when he says he measures his success, "mainly by knowing that I have done my best in each pastoral situation to present God's answer to his children's needs—he measures the real success!"[101]

Faithful Intentions Are Satisfying

Paraphrasing Samuel Johnson, William James wrote, "With mere good intentions, hell is proverbially paved." I agree with James' insertion of the word "mere" into the famous dictum by Samuel Johnson because I contend that faithful intentions do please God and that those who work them should be satisfied.

When I say that faithful intentions please God, I would not want you to think that I mean this involves wishful thinking, for that would be a uncharitable caricature of my position. What I wish you to understand is that we glorify God by our plans and work that we faithfully put into action even if those plans should eventually fail.

Do you comprehend the challenge to our faith which is involved in such cases of faithful failure? Let us say, for the sake of argument, that you have spent sixty hours of your time developing a Bible study course to meet the needs of single parent households. You have thrown yourself into this project, and it represents the very best of what you have to offer your congregation. You have also taken the trouble to work up advance publicity for your program by advertising it in your bulletin and monthly newsletter, and you have given it attention in two of your sermons. You even rearrange your schedule to give your Bible study the widest possible play, telling people that you will teach the lessons, not only on Sunday mornings, but Sunday evenings as well. And what happens? Out of a potential forty-two single parents in your parish who could certainly stand to learn something about what the Bible has to say about their situation, only four show up for the Sunday morning lesson, and three straggle in for the evening class.

How will you look at such a development as I have just described? I know how I would naturally feel. But I am convinced that I need to look past the superficial poor results and my disappointed feelings of failure and believe that, at least, my faithful intents were not wasted in the sight of God. I have to see that by faith. I must see that I have honored God and glorified him even when my faithful plans fail or give every indication of having done so. In viewing my ministerial efforts in this way, I find the strength that releases me from the trough of depression.

But I will just as quickly remind you that this must come about through a deliberate choice. As I said on p. 29 in my stated aim, "to the extent you consciously minister with God's glorification as your only goal—that you will experience a sense of accomplishment." I am saying that you must force yourself to believe and, therefore, see that what ordinarily appears as a failure actually accomplished something wonderful—God received some glory from you.

I admit, however, that it is extremely difficult to view my faithful intentions as successes in God's estimation when people treat them as obvious failures. Sure I can make it sound good when I tell you that—when your time or talents impress you as having been wasted on a project—satisfaction will well up within you if you only picture Jesus with a smile on his face, and you imagine him with a look which says: "I know, old boy, you tried, and I appreciate your efforts, though your people consider you a bumbling fool." When you feel your insides twisted in knots because your faithful intentions have been crushed by unsympathetic people or greeted with a polite "Ho-Hum," believe me, it gets discouraging. And all the fine and correctly phrased, spiritual formulas will not automatically get you out of feeling that way by merely recalling the equation to mind. I would, however, have you remember how saints greater than we struggled to maintain the beatific vision when the unfinished business and failed objectives of their ministries plunged them into depression and despair.

Elijah's Depression

In Chapter 7, I pointed out that the prophet Elijah, after he won his victory over the heathen priests at Mt. Carmel, failed to sway the bulk of his countrymen back to faithfulness to God. Instead he reaped the hate and treachery of his country's leaders. The "I am the only one left" mentality of Elijah, I suspect, also takes up residence in many of our hearts when our plans have been made and carried out faithfully, only to see them apparently fail. I remember vividly how a colleague made plans aimed at improving his church's stewardship. He built his campaign around a sermon series, but the results left him feeling ill; the Sunday after the series ended saw his church's contributions drop!

John the Baptist's Imprisonment

John's question to Jesus, "Are you the one who was to come, or should we expect someone else?" (Luke 7:19) has puzzled people through the ages. Ylvisaker writes, "What is John's motive in sending the two disciples to Jesus with this question? The exegetes are not agreed."[102]

The disagreement arises because many Christians think it's simply incredible that someone of heroic stature like John the Baptist could have harbored doubts about Jesus after he had spent so much time and energy promoting him. Ylvisaker, however, calls attention to the explanation offered by many (Godet, Daechsel, Bugge, Zahn) for John's question—that his imprisonment had flooded him with doubts: "During this period of suffering in body and soul, he was unable to cling to Jesus as the Savior of his soul. The coming of Jesus did not, in fact, harmonize with his expectations. He did not bring about the crisis among the people of the Kingdom which he had hoped for. He did not come with the flood of the Spirit and with the fire of judgment so that they could be seen."[103]

Ylvisaker himself maintains that "there is no psychological reason why John, albeit the greatest born of a woman, should not sink into doubt and misgiving."[104] What psychology could explain John's doubt? It appeared, from all outward signs, that John's ministry had ended in failure. He had been imprisoned for his zeal to do the Lord's will, and it seems likely that Christ's own behavior failed to mesh with his expectations of what a Savior was supposed to do.

Had John, of course, been able to see the future glory and triumph of the victorious and resurrected Jesus of Nazareth, one can safely assume that he would have seen his efforts as work which would eventually succeed. That would have made him happy and satisfied even there in the midst of the loneliness of his cell. This, however, is the very nub of the issue. As faith appropriates what God freely gives sinners in Christ, so faith transcends the limited abilities of native, human senses, to see that its faithful efforts really do work the invisible accomplishment of glorifying God in heaven. Working God's glorification and seeing that this has actually happened both boil down to matters of faith, a fact which presents itself as much a challenge for us as for heroes of the faith.

Faithful Intentions Encourage Ministers to Work

I keep my morale high when my intentions and efforts meet with failure or mixed results by deliberately (MAKING IT A POINT TO) reminding myself that my faithful inten-

139

tions work God's glorification. They work his glorification because my faithful efforts constitute a form of worship. I would not be doing what I am doing for God and his church except that I love him for my creation and salvation, and I wish to worship him. So long as I know that my faith in God, reacting to his glorious grace, prompted my actions, I can feel a sense of satisfaction in having worked, at the very least, God's glorification through my faithful intentions.

Working God's glorification through my faithful efforts and intentions also encourages me to go on, to continue to offer my faithful efforts in my capacity as a pastor. Failure can make a minister timid and hesitant to initiate new plans. But, knowing that my faithful intentions work God's glorification, I feel less fear now to initiate something. I can hear some saying that such an attitude might well propel me into foolish or ill-advised ventures. I will admit that I am bolder now than when I started out in the ministry. But I would also add that the opposite extreme poses an even greater danger, lack of action due to a littleness of faith. If you or I, as pastors, are to be faulted for any extreme which originates from faith and from our attempts to win glory for God, then let the criticism be that we dared too much in the name of Christ.

I offer the example of Johann Sebastian Bach. As I look at his accomplishments and the attitude with which he went about creating his works of enduring art, I find the following equation at work: a first-rate goal (working God's glorification) produces first-rate results (good works). Bach didn't give one Saxon hoot for what his critics thought of his music. This accounts for much of his trouble with the church council at St. Thomas Church in Leipzig where he ministered. As Bach plainly stated in his published music, he wrote and played to glorify God. His scores were often prefaced soli deo gloria. I see this as a clue that explains the burning drive in Bach's soul—a drive which brought out the best he had to offer and which contributed to the eventual recognition of his labors as being that of a genius.[105] I repeat my belief: first-rate goals produce first-rate results because they encourage first-rate efforts.

When you and I minister to glorify God alone, we can believe that our ministrations have produced something of lasting, eternal consequence: we have worshiped God, and this is an accomplishment which lasts. To labor in such a spirit will bring out the best in anyone who "struggles" (Colossians 1:29) in the parish ministry. It will encourage us to keep on laboring even when we feel ourselves burdened by the pressures of unfinished, never-ending tasks and failed objectives.

As I conclude this chapter, I do not want to leave you with the impression that I have perfected this ability to the point where I see all my ministerial efforts from the eternal perspective of God's glorification. I do claim, however, some growth in this area, especially as I look back on the personal successes and discouragements I have experienced as a parish pastor. I say this as an encouragement to other pastors who, like myself, might be prone to putting too much stock in trying to measure the effectiveness of their ministries by the vagaries of outward, visible results. Make the glorification of God the ultimate goal of all your labors. See your labors actually accomplishing this objective, and notice two things happening. You will sense not only a growing satisfaction with your ministry, but you will also gain the confidence to put forth first-rate efforts, because you know that you are producing first-rate results—your faith sees that your labors have glorified God.

Summary

1. Because the work of the ministry deals with matters of the soul, ministers are left to measure the success of

141

their efforts by the fruits of faith in their parishioners' lives.

2. Ministers are task oriented in defining the purpose of their work. When ministers attempt to measure how successful their work has been in and on the lives of their parishioners, they will find barriers like time and space hindering their ability to determine the long-term results of such work.

3. Ministers should take heart in knowing that their faithful labors and even their faithful intentions result in an immediate accomplishment, the glorification of God, because faithful labors and intentions are a form of worship. This should prove satisfying to ministers when they fail to see visible results from their labors, or when they see their faithful intentions end in apparent failure.

4. The more a minister grows convinced that his faithful labors work the first-rate goal of glorifying God, the more he will find himself willing to put forth first-rate efforts, producing first-rate results.

Advice

1. Read F. LaGard Smith's *Fallen Shepherds Scattered Sheep*, Chapter 3, "How the Mighty Are Fallen." Smith has some good insights into the inherent dangers of the public ministry, in which pastors labor in the pomp and circumstance of the worship setting. Ministers find themselves in the limelight and must guard against abusing this privilege.

2. How are you fixed for hobbies? People like us who work in such a nebulous area like that of the soul need some sort of diversion where we can satisfy our longing to see something concretely accomplished. Call it therapy; I call it model-railroading. I worry about some of the men I encounter in the ministry who impress me as all work

and no play. They get so myopic about their parish tasks that I fear they loose perspective and are always straining to see and find what they have accomplished, but they can't see the proverbial forest for the trees. If you resist calling yourself a workaholic but nonetheless recognize that I am describing you, and if you have no real hobbies whereby you can see little things accomplished, consider backing off from what I suspect is your overly crowded schedule. Go to the library, and get some ideas on how to spend an hour or two "constructively" in your basement, yard, or garage. Do something on a weekly basis.

3. One veteran pastor told me early on in my ministry, "You have to get used to the feeling that much of your work will never be done." I have reconciled myself to the feeling, and I no longer feel so guilty. Have you reconciled yourself to that feeling?

Endnotes

[84] Nathan R. Pope, "Opinion Poll of Select Protestant Clergymen of the Greater Milwaukee Area," (Racine, Wisconsin: personal research for Major Writing Project, Luther Rice Seminary Doctor of Ministry program, (1 June 1989), 5.

[85] Ibid., 9.

[86] Ibid., 4.

[87] Ibid., 7.

[88] Ibid., 11.

[89] Nathan R. Pope, "Survey of Students of Wisconsin Lutheran Seminary," (Racine, Wisconsin: personal research for Major Writing Project, Luther Rice Seminary Doctor of Ministry program, June 1, 1989), 1.

[90] Ibid., 4.

[91] Ibid., 6.

[92] Ibid., 7.

[93] Ibid., 8.

[94] Ibid., 15.

[95] Ibid., 18.

[96] Ibid., 21.

[97] Ibid., passim.

[98] Pope, "Opinion Poll of Select Protestant Clergymen of the Greater Milwaukee Area," passim.

[99] Kadel, *Growth in Ministry*, 66.

[100] Ibid.

[101] Pope, "Opinion Poll of Select Protestant Clergymen of the Greater Milwaukee Area," 6.

[102] Johann Ylvisaker, *The Gospels* (Minneapolis: Augsburg Publishing House, 1932), 302.

[103] Ibid.

[104] Ibid., 303.

CHAPTER 9
LACK OF
APPRECIATION

Ministers Need to Feel Appreciated

Human beings will generally perform the toughest, dirtiest, and most difficult tasks as long as they feel that others appreciate and approve of their work. This same principle also applies to us who have been called to undertake an extremely difficult and serious business. We, too, like, and, yes, need to feel appreciated.

Ministers Have the World's Most Important Work

In a day and age in which the secularization of American society continues unabated and the importance of the church and its ministry seemingly has been diminished, perhaps, we ministers need to stop and wonder about the dimensions of our work. Just how important is the Christian ministry anyway?

The programs that march across our television screens inform us that the world, for the most part, sees our work as ministers as trivial and irrelevant. Other professionals can tune in and watch their work being glamorized and, perhaps, even depicted as glorious and exciting. But the ministry? The impression is usually given that men of the cloth, caring and clever individuals that they may be, have little worthwhile work to do and that they have even less influence.

While this may be the perception of those who are caught in the grip of spiritual blindness and do not value the things of God and eternity, the fact is that we pastors have been entrusted with the world's most important work. Yes, the ministry of preaching the everlasting gospel continues as the world's most serious and important work simply because the world of eternity, whether some like it or not or believe it or not, awaits all men.

Sacrificing for Ungrateful Sheep

Ministers make many sacrifices in order to shepherd their flocks. Their salaries, compared with those of other white-collar professionals, remain low. Their work hours, on the other hand, remain long and unpredictable. This sacrifice of time and money on their part impacts their personal lives and their families. And when they do not receive at least some appreciation for the sacrifices they have made, it frequently breeds bitterness and resentment. Yes, pastors understand when they enter the ministry that they are making this sacrifice of time and money voluntarily. But it still proves stressful when these sacrifices, made on behalf of King and kingdom, are treated indifferently by others.

Our feelings are hurt when we detect a lack of appreciation for our work. We may, for example, have parceled out food, food certificates, and even rent money to needy people of the community but did not receive even one note of thanks from them or anyone else. Certainly we are troubled

146

when we encounter such an air of ingratitude. We never get used to. It hurts deeply.

But such a spirit of ingratitude on the part of our parishioners can create an even bigger problem. It can dampen a minister's enthusiasm for his vocation—and that very enthusiasm is part and parcel of ministerial competency. Pastoral competency, as I defined it in Chapter One, is the refusal to give up when things get tough. And life does get tough when the sheep withhold their approval for the shepherd's work. Ungrateful parishioners can pose serious roadblocks for ministerial competency. Some men can take only so much after they have continually given of themselves, sometimes even unwittingly having put their vocations ahead of their families. When they experience ingratitude, they may wonder why they should have to take such treatment in view of the sacrifices they have made. As a result some have simply packed it in and quit.

When the Sheep Persecute the Shepherd

Ingratitude takes many forms. There is the silent variety—the "thank-you" that never comes, the compliment that is never spoken, the congratulation that is withheld. With that sort of ingratitude I have no major problem, except that occasionally my feelings get bruised. But there is also a spirit of ingratitude which comes across as hostile, angry, hateful. That kind I find difficult to forget, much less easily cast off emotionally. When, for example, people not only fail to appreciate the help or advice I have offered but also go on to express open hostility toward me, then I am deeply troubled. And I could seriously imagine myself quitting if I were subjected to enough of this sort of treatment— for want of a better term, let's label it persecution.

Persecution, the worst form ingratitude can take, is the most serious roadblock in the way of carrying out that aspect of ministerial competency which involves refusing to give up. Such persecution saps enthusiasm and drives ministers out of the ministry.

Whether the blows are laid on with sticks or with words, persecution stings. Church finances can distract and trouble, scandals and tragedies among parishioners can cause sleepless nights, and disagreements over congregational policy can irritate, but, as far as I am concerned, persecutions—that is, personal attacks which come from my own parishioners—have done the most to disturb my mental and emotional tranquillity. Ironically, the average American minister experiences the greatest share of persecution from the very flock that he has been called to shepherd.

Now, I wish to make myself absolutely clear. When I use the word *persecution*, I am not referring to the ordinary criticism you and I hear, with or without our invitation, in the course of carrying out our many tasks. True, some of this criticism, in the process of discussion and debate, can be heated. True, we may even feel ourselves under attack. But that is not what I am referring to when I use the word persecution.

For example, some years ago I was speaking about new Bible translations at a meeting of senior citizens. I was asked why the King James Version had been scraped in favor of a newer version. My answer—that language changes made this move necessary—proved unconvincing to this elderly jury. In fact, they then used this occasion as a stepping stone to raise all sorts of grievances against me for all the other changes that had taken place since my arrival in the parish. Like a failed vaudevillian dodging the audience's ripe tomatoes, I quickly found myself fending off a flurry of attacks. Believe me, I felt the sting of those criticisms. But, had I been persecuted? No.

When I use the word persecution, I'm talking about actions which reveal an active or aggressive rejection of God and his Word. Under this definition I would include such things as active resistance, back-talk, disrespect, gossip, guff, slander, law suits, and physical attacks.

For instance, a minister who gets punched in the nose by an angry parishioner who rejects the minister's sound doctrine or practice has experienced persecution, admittedly an extreme form of persecution. When he discovers that other parishioners sympathize with the man who threw the punch, he may, in fact, feel as if he wants to quit.

There was a minister who found himself in just such a situation—in a fist-fight at the entrance to a cemetery with a group of mourners who vehemently disapproved of the way the minister had conducted the funeral service. Later they succeeded in driving him out of the church. Would you not call that a case of persecution?

I wince at the thought of the possibility of someone landing a punch on my nose. Yet, as I look back on certain episodes in my ministry, I wonder just how close I came to collecting one. I know that I have made enemies because I have condemned people's sins or faulted them for their misbehavior or disagreed with their heresies. And I have paid the price for my actions—finding myself out of favor with them and their families. You may have felt that sting too.

When such enemies act out their disfavor and set out to injure us by their words or actions or to ruin our reputations or to discredit our authority and effectiveness, we will feel that as the worst form of ingratitude. You know the feeling—you try to do what you believe is right, and you get crucified for it. Remind you of anyone to whom that happened? You are not alone; he knows how you feel.

Persecution, however, comes with the territory; you cannot be a man of God and escape persecution. Jesus predicted this treatment for his ministers on earth: "I am sending you out like sheep among wolves. Therefore be as shrewd as snakes and as innocent as doves. But be on your guard against men; they will hand you over to the local councils and flog you in their synagogues" (Matthew 10:16,17).

Ministers Need Encouragement

A whole industry has grown up around the contemporary problem of burnout. We are told that everyone is burning out, and workshop upon seminar (did Paul ever attend one of these?) warns us that ministers should recognize themselves as potential candidates.

Many diagnoses have been offered to explain this phenomenon and its causes. G. Lloyd Rediger, author of *Coping with Clergy Burnout*, supplies his readers with an inventory of twenty-five factors through which a do-it-yourselfer can determine whether or not he is a candidate for burnout.[105]

Burnout undoubtedly results from a number of spiritual, emotional, and psychological factors. Common sense tells me that many men become dispirited or demoralized through some combination of hard work, self-sacrifice, and lack of appreciation—a lack of appreciation which expresses itself either in a silent fashion or in the form of persecution.

Robert Michel, director of Wisconsin Lutheran Child and Family Service of Milwaukee, told pastors in a clinical letter, "In his subsequent dialogue with Jehovah at Mount Horeb, Elijah manifests several more typical characteristics of burn-out. He reminds God that he has been *very zealous in the Lord's service*, showing a sense of bitterness at the *level of appreciation* the people—and perhaps God himself—are showing. Further, he reveals the burnout's typical feeling of indispensability—that he alone is serving God: 'I, even I only, am left.'"

We ministers would like to feel and need to feel appreciated for the hard and important work we perform. Where do we find such appreciation?

Winning Approval by Glorifying Things Rather Than God

Too many ministers in the 20th century Christian church have turned their calling into a gargoyled ministry. No longer content to save souls, they have thrown themselves into causes and crusades which bear no similarity to the mission which once brought St. Boniface from Devonshire to Hesse—to fell Thor's sacred oak.

Today's erstwhile missionaries preach ecology, stage gay rights parades, lobby for socialistic welfare programs, promote abortion rights, meddle in international politics, and cozy up to secular humanism. And we need not wonder how things have reached this state when we hear them proclaim that mankind no longer has a sinful problem which needs remedying. The words of one popular preacher sum it all up for these terribly misguided individuals: "I don't think anything has been done in the name of Christ . . . that has proven more destructive to human personality, and hence counterproductive to the evangelistic enterprise, than the unchristian, uncouth strategy of attempting to make people aware of their lost and sinful condition."[106]

Had these preachers accompanied Boniface to the Frisians, they probably would have carved their initials into the woodsy idols instead of making them feel the bite of their axes.

Why do these ministers follow such a program? Why do they crusade for every cause except the one which consumed the lives of the apostles like Paul, who wrote: "For I resolved to know nothing while I was with you except Jesus Christ and him crucified" (1 Corinthians 2:2).

The ills besetting the misguided clergy of this or any age are caused, of course, by the devil and the world. But I also see dark forces at work within their own sinful hearts. For example, the desire to win approval or appreciation from people for the investment of one's time and efforts is one of the culprits that tempts some ministers to shirk their responsibilities to preach law and gospel. How this natural desire to feel appreciation goes awry is demonstrated in the following Pauline warning: "But even if we or an angel from heaven should preach a gospel other than the one we preached to you, let him be eternally condemned! As we have already said, so now I say again: If anybody is preaching to you a gospel other than what you accepted, let him be eternally condemned! Am I now trying to win the approval of men, or of God? Or am I trying to please men? If I were still trying to please men, I would not be a servant of Christ" (Galatians 1:8-10).

Paul identifies the germ of sin behind apostasy as the desire to win approval, the approval of the wrong party—the approval of men rather than of God. The temptation to please people, even if it means diluting law and gospel, reveals itself as a permanent feature in a sinful world. And since the ministry is a people business, we understand why it happens. The approval of people shows itself in visible and tangible ways; the approval of God remains invisible.

Playing to the crowd, however, fails to glorify God even if, for the time, it makes a minister feel worthwhile, appreciated, and useful when he does it.

Watering Down the Word to Win Approval

You and I feel the temptation to turn ourselves into men-pleasers in the day-to-day grind of parish experience. In the pursuit of making our people happy, as we work and walk among them, we face the constant temptation to exchange God's glory for our own by compromising his word. John Jeske, professor of Old Testament at Wisconsin Lutheran Seminary, told the delegates of the 1989 Convention of the Wisconsin Ev. Lutheran Synod, "The man in the pulpit is not immune to the fear of man. He has regularly to speak to people already knocked around by life. He doesn't want to add more hurt. He wants to be liked."

To win people's approval, ministers may become soft on sin, or they may even hedge on the divinity of Christ. They may water down the gospel in order to play to the universalists in their crowd. Or, they may pose as spiritual sugar daddies, promising their flock material or health benefits in exchange for their love gifts of money. Moral and confessional cowardice has many far reaching tentacles, and I think a convincing case can be made that many of them can be traced to the desire which loves "praise from men more than praise from God" (John 12:43).

Watering Down Practice to Win Approval

Doctrine and practice are supposed to be connected, the latter proceeding from the former. But we all know how easy it is to preach correct doctrine from the protective confines of the pulpit, and how much more difficult it is to translate doctrine into practice in the tense setting of a personal confrontation.

"Pastor, I've been a member of this church all my life, and you're telling me that my son can't get married in this church because you say he has an unscriptural divorce? How would you like me to take my offerings some place else?"

"Why can't I take communion in your church? I'm not of your faith, as you put it, pastor, but I am a Christian, and I used to belong here years ago before you became the minister."

"Pastor, when my daughter gets married in our church next year, she would like you to do her fiancee a favor. You know that he's Jewish, don't you? Well, would it hurt if his rabbi had a little prayer during the service? His side belongs to the Reformed synagogue, and they're a bit looser than the Orthodox, I hear, and according to my daughter's fiancee, the rabbi would be willing to take part if you're willing. What should I tell my daughter?"

People today are not exactly shy about putting questions like these to you and to me. We live in a different age, an age where false ecumenicism and doctrinal indifference and moral laxity cause some people to ask things of their pastors which their grandparents would never have dreamed of doing. And when these people fail to get their way, they threaten to boycott their minister's sermons or transfer their allegiance and money elsewhere—tempting situations, would you not say?

God Approves of and Appreciates Those Who Glorify Him

If you have ever found yourself downcast or discouraged after encountering such ungrateful people or after experiencing some form of persecution, how closely have you identified with our Lord and the circumstances under which he labored? How much comfort have you drawn from the way he found the encouragement to go forward in his ministry?

How could Jesus, humanly speaking now, have kept up his efforts to continue his ministry despite the opposition which mounted against him? On what power did he draw when people showed him such ungrateful attitudes or when they persecuted him or when they conspired against him?

Would you agree with me that his goal of saving sinners kept Jesus from quitting his ministry? Might you not also concur that his mercy (Luke 19:9,10) fueled his desire to complete his saving mission? I believe that Christ's power, which enabled him to persevere in the face of terrible opposition, emanated from his grace. His grace, his mercy, his pity for sinners compelled and propelled him onwards towards his goal of winning salvation for all men. And we love to dwell on that motivation, do we not? We love to picture Jesus pressing forward, fingers punctured with slivers, hands wrestling with his cross, legs wobbling, now bending, stumbling, stooping, picking himself up—we see him force himself to the site of his execution, his execution for us.

But did not Jesus also do what he did for someone else, namely, for his Father? Was not Jesus motivated to fulfill his mission because he also sought to win for his Father the glory of salvation (John 17:4)? And because Jesus came to work the will of his Father (John 4:34), can we not say that Jesus was motivated to fulfill his mission, despite the opposition he faced, because he enjoyed his Father's authorization?

God's Approval of His Son

How? How did Jesus enjoy the authorization of his heavenly Father?

When Jesus entered into his public ministry, remember the send-off which his Father gave him. There at his baptism the Father gave his Son the public credentials to legitimize the claim which Jesus would make on the hearts and consciences of people. And, recall that his enemies challenged Jesus on this critical issue: "'Tell us by what authority you are doing these things,' they said. 'Who gave you this authority?'" (Luke 20:2).

And now I arrive at my point. Jesus went into this critical, difficult, terribly controversial public phase of his ministry with his Father's authority. What did this authorization translate into?

Approval. Appreciation. "This is my Son, whom I love; with him I am *well pleased*" (Matthew 3:17).

Thus, whenever God's Son would find himself out of favor with the public, he would still know that he had his Father's approval. And I submit that this approval or appreciation from his Father dramatically figured into Christ's staying abilities when no one else was there to stand with him (Matthew 26:56). Jesus could face the mob armed with stones (John 10:33), could stand his ground against armed soldiers (John 18:3-6), could go it alone against rigged courts (John 18:20), and could face his Father's damning hatred of sin which he willingly bore in his body and soul (Mark 15:34), because he knew he still had his Father's approval and appreciation for what he did: "The one who sent me is with me; he has not left me alone, for I always do what pleases him" (John 8:29).

Because Jesus did what he did for God's glory, he never experienced self-doubt or pitied himself for all the trouble his ministry brought him. And I submit that Jesus' example illustrates for us the best way to handle or combat the ingratitude or persecution we periodically face. Despite the frequent ingratitude and persecution shown to him by some of those very people he came to seek and to save, Jesus finished his course because he enjoyed his Father's approval.

Do you?

The more you and I seek to glorify our heavenly Father for his grace and mercy—so free and so full—the more will we feel his pleasure and approval. And the more we feel our Father's pleasure and approval, the more our desire will grow to endure in our ministries, to finish the course, to better our abilities, and to be happy that Someone is happy with us.

Glorifying God Pleases Him

It makes me feel important to know that my faithful labors and my faithful intentions please and glorify God. In view of what his grace has done for me and for you, God seeks, yes, expects love and appreciation in return from us. Worship. Worship with lip and life. That is what he expects. And we can feel happy to do what pleases him.

I want to take this matter of pleasing God one step further. If glorifying God makes us happy and causes us to feel important because what we are doing pleases him, then these positive results will also prove to be an incentive for us to work God's glorification even more. But, please, understand what I am saying in the spirit that I say it. I do not mean that we want to glorify God in order to manufacture a sense of importance and happiness in or for ourselves, or as if our feelings are the chief thing; God's feelings stand preeminent. No, I mean that doing what God intended us to do—that is, working his glorification by faith as our worshipful response to his grace—fills us with positive feelings indirectly. And people will always work their best at anything which gives them happiness and fulfills them.

We ministers must believe that God does see our faithful intentions and efforts. In fact, we must grow in our belief that God loves these products of our faith and that he does so whether or not our parishioners do. When we believe that we have worked God's glorification and that God finds pleasure in our intentions and efforts, we will be heartened and encouraged by this knowledge. I hold up the Apostle Paul as a supreme example of this fact. Imprisoned by the authorities for his preaching and attacked by false brothers for his apostolic claims, Paul rose above discouragement. He rejoiced to do what he knew was benefiting and pleasing God: "I eagerly expect and hope that I will in no way be ashamed, but will have sufficient courage so that now as always Christ will be exalted in my body, whether by life or by death. For to me, to live is Christ and to die is gain" (Philippians 1:20,21).

Incredible but inspiring. Human approval was not the underlying motive for Paul's intentions and labors. Rather, he sought God's pleasure and placed the highest value on accomplishing that: "So we make it our goal to please him [Jesus], whether we are at home in the body or away from it" (2 Corinthians 5:9).

Minister soli deo gloria. Know that every task you perform in the spirit of this goal hits the mark. Believe that God is pleased with you, and you, like Paul, will experience a heightened sense of dedication. Know that you have God's approval, as Jesus could claim, and you will possess the power to press forward with your ministry to sinners, whether they are appreciative or not.

"On the contrary, we speak as men approved by God to be entrusted with the gospel. We are not trying to please men but God, who tests our hearts" (1 Thessalonians 2:4).

Faith Creates Approval

Faith saves sinners. Faith also puts sinful human existence into focus. When humans repent of their sins and come to believe that they have forgiveness in Christ, then, and only then, do they find true purpose. They live to give God glory (sanctification), and to the extent that they consciously set out to do that, they soar to individual heights of happiness in knowing that God feels pleased to accept their sacrifices of faith. How much more applicable is this to the man whose profession makes him responsible for the public administration of faith.

Early on in his life a boy named Paul wanted to enter the ministry. It was not until he was 44, however, that Paul saw his dream come true. He was ordained into the ministry in a small city church. There he settled into his calling, found a wife, and began a family.

But, Paul's happiness proved short-lived. A jealous colleague caused him much unpleasantness. Relief came when Paul was called to a big city church, where he served as an assistant pastor. Paul distinguished himself as a first-rate homiletician, and he soon won for himself the reputation as the city's most popular preacher.

But trouble once again found Paul. This time church politics reared its ugly head. Paul's superiors demanded that he compromise his doctrinal position. Paul refused. As a result he was forced to resign. Incredibly, just before this battle with his superiors took place, Paul had suffered a great personal loss. Three of his five children had died tragically. And no sooner was he deposed from his call than a fourth child died. Then his wife fell seriously ill.

Taken aback by all of Paul's tragedies, Paul's superiors allowed him to retain his position in the church. Yet when it once again became apparent that Paul, despite all his sorrows, was still unwilling to water down his doctrinal integrity, he was forced to resign his call a second time. Then, on Easter, his wife died. Only Paul and his six-year-old son remained. Influenced by Paul's friends and supporters, a church in a neighboring city called Paul as their pastor, and there he served for seven years before his death.

So reads the incredible life of Paul Gerhardt (1607-1676), a man with a true pastor's heart and one of the best, if not the best, of all the hymn writers of the Lutheran church. Read his life's story, feel his pain, sing his hymns ("Rejoice my heart, be glad and sing", "Why should cross and trial grieve me?", "Awake my heart with gladness" to name but a few), and you will not find anything even close to the "golly-gee-whiz-do-I-have-it-tough" mentality that has descended on the American ministry.

Consider, minister, your tasks and assignments, your efforts, your painful sacrifices in the name of God.

You have spent four hours in the nursing homes, calling upon the Alzheimer victim, the lonely widow, the bored to death. You reminded them of God's love.

You have visited with a new family that has moved into the neighborhood. You hope that they will see things your way and join your church.

You have counseled twice with a young couple in love. They are living together, but they remain unmarried. Will they act upon what you have told them about separating?

You have confirmed a class of twelve eighth graders whom you have instructed the past two years in catechism class. You pray that they will remain faithful.

You have preached. You have taught. You have counseled. You have visited. You have explained. You have admonished. You have prayed. You have encouraged. You have witnessed to the truth of God.

Has it done any good?

Do your people approve? Are the people upon whom you have spent your time and faith appreciative? Always?

Weigh your motives for ministry.

Why do you expend your time and effort as a pastor? Are you, at least to some degree, trying to win favor from people? Could it be possible that in some small way you are seeking to establish your own importance? Are you the kind of person who has sleepless nights because you have seen your special efforts or your grand successes greeted with silence? Do you consider yourself a successful pastor? Do people tell you that they regard you as a successful pastor, or do they mainly direct your attention to the negatives in your ministry?

Minister to people graciously, and do it soli Deo gloria. Feel, yes, feel appreciated by God, if you have, indeed, ministered to his glory alone. Be convinced of God's approval. See him smiling on you, and know that his approval means more than anything else. And in this process of feeling, convincing, seeing, and knowing, experience the motivation to do even better what you are doing. The dynamics of this are easily understood as Reginald McDonough points out in *Working with Volunteer Leaders in the Church*, "Perhaps nothing builds motivation more than to know that someone we respect appreciates us as persons and appreciates the work we are doing."[107] How much more true if we change the "*someone*" to God and also change our relationship to him to one of fear, love, and trust in him.

You will not please everyone in your ministrations. In fact, you may even anger people when you do everything correctly; Jesus did (John 8:46), and some hated him for it.

Accordingly, how can you, the servant who is not above his master, expect to win everyone's approval? You will displease some; you will encounter ingratitude and disapproval from others, and the resulting feeling of discouragement will hurt.

How do you and I handle the hurt and the discouragement? We can, of course, read a book or attend a workshop to gain understanding and insight. But ultimately we will find our greatest source of strength in encountering the living Christ through faith, petitioning him to take away the hurt of disapproval. Yes, we will find new strength in the Savior's approval of our work. You and I, then, constantly need to refocus our feelings and thoughts on the reason we have become what we are and on the reason we continue to do what we do—to serve our fellow man so that we might work the glory of God, knowing that God appreciates it.

Believe that God loves your faithful efforts and intentions and that he derives pleasure from them. Feel his appreciation. See it for what it is, an exercise of faith, just like everything else in your ministry. "Whatever you do, work at it with all your heart, as working for the Lord, not for men, knowing that you will receive an inheritance from the Lord as a reward. It is the Lord Christ you are serving" (Colossians 3:23,24). We serve King and kingdom! We are appreciated!

Summary

1. Christian ministers have the most important vocation in the world. They also make personal sacrifices for the flock because of their desire to minister. A common temptation under these circumstances asks pastors why they should continue in their work, much less strive to do it better, when their peoples' response to their efforts can be so underwhelming that it comes across as thanklessness or worse, as persecution.

2. Because approval is important, ministers may be tempted to change or water down the Word of God or compromise ethical and confessional practice in order to avoid disapproval and to curry favor with parishioners.

3. God approves of those who walk in his truth and seek to please him through their faithful efforts. Ministers will work, not as though they are serving men, but the Lord Jesus and strive for that which pleases him. As ministers believe this, they will experience the approval and appreciation they need, and they will receive from the one whose pleasure counts, namely, God.

Advice

1. How well do you know yourself? If you would be inclined to compromise yourself vocationally to avoid displeasure or persecution, are you more likely to compromise doctrine by omitting to speak on certain subjects, or are you more likely to compromise practice by omitting to perform certain actions? Think back on your ministerial experiences. Can you think of an instance where you compromised your religious convictions to avoid someone's disapproval? Did you do this when you were relatively inexperienced or later on in your ministry? Did this experience strengthen your resolve to refuse to compromise your convictions in subsequent, similar circumstances, or did this experience spook you enough to make you avoid the circumstances which would force you to choose between wanting to please men or God?

2. I know a small number of ministers who have sought a vote of confidence from their congregations. How do you feel about such tests? If your work and results came up for review annually, how would such a test or vote of confidence affect your performance in your current ministry? Would the prospect of such an annual test increase

your accountability to the congregation, or would it make you more cautious or more timid or more politically minded in your work?

Endnotes

[105] Rediger has many descriptions of the symptoms of burnout, citing the causative and symptomatic features of burnout. See G. Lloyd Rediger, *Coping with Clergy Burnout* (Valley Forge, Pennsylvania: Judson Press, 1982), 48-50.

[106] Michael Horton, *Agony of Deceit*, 78.

[107] Reginald M. McDonough, *Working with Volunteer Leaders in the Church* (Nashville: Abingdon Press, 1988), 121,122.

CHAPTER 10 ACKNOWLEDG-ING SUCCESS

Success, Failure, and Self-Destruction

When I was installed into a new congregation in 1980, the preacher, my uncle Reginald, ominously pointed his finger at me from the pulpit and thundered, "You are a marked man." Each time he repeated the phrase I imagined his words burning one huge bullseye into the back of my head, and that the eyes of the worshipers, directed by his words, were aimed there. When the service was over, I felt awfully conspicuous as I walked down the aisle to greet the people at the doors. I imagined that all my secret thoughts stood exposed and available for inspection, much like a dirty sock turned inside out.

I try to wear this "You are a marked man" label of Christian ministry in connection with every facet of my labors, knowing that people are, indeed, watching and observing me. "You are a marked man" speaks to all of us in the ministry, warning us to put ourselves on guard, for we know that people carefully evaluate how we act and conduct ourselves, and that they quickly make book on our habits and characteristics. And when our people really get to know us, they may even be able to predict our moves. I still have to chuckle as I remember Irwin Habeck, my professor of homiletics, joking about a certain preacher, whose predilection for filling his sermons with clichés was so habitual and repetitive that during the services the schoolboys would make friendly bets as to where and when they would appear.

"You are a marked man" also warns each of us to develop a keen awareness of our behavior. How well do we know our habits and tendencies? How accurately can we predict the way we will react under certain conditions in our ministries? How honestly have we come to know and "mark" ourselves?

How, for example, do you handle success in ministry?

What happens to you when you succeed?

I have come to the point where I mark my successes in ministry "potentially hazardous to spirituality," much as I might put the same label on my failures. I would never have said such a thing during my school days or in the salad days of my ministry. But today, if I had the chance to reprise Tony Randall's role in Frank Tashlin's 1957 hit, "Will Success Spoil Rock Hunter?" I think I would cast Randall as a struggling minister catapulted into televangelist fame instead of as a copywriter promoted to managing director of an ad agency as the original script called for. The change in character would be appropriate because this cinematic moral work shows how a man can be tempted, in fact, nearly ruined, by success.

Ruined by success? Is that far fetched? My own experience and my observation of the tragic downfalls of other pastors has convinced me to be as wary of my successes as my failures, because success has impressed me as a condition which creates its own unique temptations for sin. I am a marked man in this sense, because I have marked myself.

Some Ministers Are Unable to Stand Success

Believing that ministerial success can translate into as potentially ruinous a situation as failure places us in an ironic set of circumstances. It's ironic because our seminaries taught us to strive for excellence in our ministrations, and excellence, I believe, comes about as one of those natural by-products from pursuing any vocation soli deo gloria (see pp. 140,141 on first-rate goals producing first-rate results).

But you and I will also recognize that excellence forms a two-edged sword. It can be used to strike out and win great glories for God, but it can also turn on those who wield it in a vainglorious way. Our age has witnessed so many successful preachers—whether merely hometown celebrities or media stars—fall from their pedestals that we can ill afford to dismiss, out of hand, the warning of the Lord delivered through the Apostle Paul: "So, if you think you are standing firm, be careful that you don't fall" (1 Corinthians 10:12).

Richard Dortch, one-time sidekick to the toppled head of the PTL Club, Jim Bakker, confessed in *Christianity Today* that he and others had a problem in defining and handling success: "Sometimes I think the church doesn't know anything about true success. It's all tied to how many stations we have in our network, or how big our building is. It's easy to lose control, to compromise without recognizing it. At PTL there was no time taken for prayer or for family, because the show had to go on. We were so caught up in God's work that we forgot about God. It took the tragedy, the kick in the teeth, to bring us to our senses."[108]

How tragic when ministers misdefine success or seek it for the wrong reasons. How odd when they mismanage triumphs into failures. Much has been made of the failures of the televangelists of the 1980's. At the pinnacle of success Swaggert, Bakker, and others were rocked by scandals. And then in the fall of 1991, ABC's *20/20* media magazine made additional allegations regarding the misconduct and chicanery of other nationally syndicated charismatic televangelists.

On the local level as well, almost every community has a story to tell about some ordinary, successful parish pastor who has managed to bungle his way into infamy. There's the story of Peter, a highly successful senior minister, who pastored a large metropolitan church. At the peak of his powers, with his church enjoying unprecedented growth, the story broke that Peter was involved in an extra-marital affair with the wife of one of the church's officers. Peter resigned, claiming that he had been framed.

Everyone has heard variations of this story, for similar circumstances repeat themselves in church after church, city after city, and year after year. Sexual misconduct has probably ruined the successful careers of more men than any other cause.

You and I know of pastors who appeared to be enjoying highly successful careers, but suddenly their ministries went up in smoke. Circumstances revealed them to be adulterers, peeping Toms, thieves, child molesters, drunkards. It's almost as if some ministers could not stand their own success. Why must it happen that some ministers, enjoying at least a modicum of success, self-destruct?

Some Ministers Are Unable to Stand Failure

In his book, *What Ministers Can't Learn in Seminary*, R. Robert Cueni cites the case of a newly installed pastor who turned around a failing congregation. This congregation's attendance at worship services had been declining rapidly until the new man came. Then in a matter of months the attendance amazingly doubled. How would you have expected this pastor to have reacted to this success, to this

167

pleasant turn of events? Cueni reports that three years later the pastor resigned. Why? He believed he had failed because his own personal goals were largely unmet.[109]

Men sometimes leave the ministry because they are unwilling to accept what they perceive as failed goals. On the other hand, some ministers stubbornly refuse to resign or move to another parish, because they are unwilling to admit that they have failed. And so they mulishly attempt to hold on, subjecting the congregation to controversy, distractions, low morale, or stagnation.

Cueni explains that some ministers experience intense personal agony because they fear personal failure, and they harbor such fear because they have adopted models of success that are entirely inappropriate for the Christian ministry and because they are trying to gain a sense of self-worth by their success. I have a slightly different perspective. Could not the word *pride* be substituted for Cueni's *self-worth* as the motive for avoiding failure?

Can you believe that pride makes some ministers unable to stand success, while it makes others intolerant of failure? I characterize these proud attitudes as a "God-complex."

"You are a marked man" warns us that the ministry puts us into a tempting situation. We may feel that we are as indispensable as God, or we may wind up coveting his place among the people we serve. Those who succumb to this temptation often wake up to its self-destructive nature only after they have been laid low by the inevitable crash which comes from trying to play God. That crash comes sooner or later. Ask the devils.

Success Challenges Ministers to Be Humble

Physicians are often *accused* of "playing God" in the operating room or in other life or death situations. I do not recall hearing anyone use this expression "playing God" in connection with medical doctors except with a negative connotation, and so I use the word accuse in the above sentence with deliberate implications.

Ministers also are often accused of "playing God." The accusation usually implies that ministers have no more right to stand in the place of God than medical doctors. I have heard this criticism leveled against a parish pastor: "Who does he think he is? God?" The nature of the question indicates that the speaker felt that the minister had no business doing or saying what he believes only God should say or do.

I would contend, however, that ministers can legitimately "play God," that ministers justifiably can say or do things which some believe worthy only of God. You know what I am referring to: our calls charge us with the holy business of acting as God's vicars. The classic example of "playing God," which springs automatically to my mind, comes from the Lutheran liturgy, where the pastor, after hearing the congregation's confession of sins, announces: "Upon this your confession, I, by virtue of my office, as a called and ordained servant of the Word, announce the grace of God unto all of you, and in the stead and by the command of my Lord Jesus Christ I forgive you all your sins in the name of the Father and of the Son and of the Holy Ghost."[110]

"By virtue of my office". . . "called and ordained". . . "in the stead and by the command". . . "I forgive." We ministers function by the authority of God (1 Corinthians 12:28) and by human appointment (the diploma attesting to it is hanging stamped and framed on your study wall) to act as heaven's spiritual viceroy. Therein lies the rub; Satan, adoring fans, and the inbred hubris of our natures combine to tempt us to shuck the role of God's representative and assume the role of his replacement.

Wayne Oates warns ministers of the "ever present temptation to supplant rather than to represent God."[111] Oates accurately sizes up the situation as a contest over glorification, saying, "You as the pastor may easily be lured into *substituting your own sovereignty for that of God,* 'in order that the excellency may be of yourself rather than of God.' . . . Your relative degree of authority is derived by reason of the One whom you as pastor symbolize; therefore your *greatest temptation is to assume that it originated with yourself,* to confuse the symbolism of your role with the reality of God."[112]

Achieving success in our roles as God's representatives challenges us to remain humble. This has great bearing on the concept of ministerial competency. I offered a definition of competency previously which said that competent ministers will guard against pride and emulate the attitude of him who stooped to serve sinners. I hope you can appreciate better, now that you have read thus far, how this works into the dynamics of ministerial success, failure, and self-destruction.

The man who works to give God the glory with his efforts will have less of his ego on the line. He will weather better the storms which blow in, the storms which threaten his programs with failure, since he knows the true goals of his plans and labors: he aims to add glory, not to his own, but to God's reputation. If his plans succeed, he feels happy and satisfied, knowing that his work and motivation have hit the mark and have pleased God. If his plans fail, he knows that God congratulates him for his faithful intentions, whether his parishioners see it that way or not.

When pride rules in our hearts, we have a difficult time appreciating the importance of God's glorification. Everything hangs on this motivation. For when pride makes us so fearful of failure (as if our egos were the true goal of our labors), or when pride makes us so dissatisfied with our success (as if our egos demanded more), then we can understand why men, so motivated, find the ministry so disheartening. The ministry aims to glorify the one who emptied himself in order to stoop low for sinners. Any attitude or motivation which refuses to abide by this shepherdly spirit, implicit in the words and actions of the Son of God, will sooner or later find itself out of sync with that spirit.

The "Nebuchadnezzar" Syndrome

Accomplishments war against humility. Achievements can be turned into objects of worship. Observe Nebuchadnezzar as a representative of the proud heart adoring its own successes.

Daniel records the extent of Nebuchadnezzar's self-glorification: "As the king was walking on the roof of the royal palace of Babylon, he said, 'Is not this the great Babylon I have built as the royal residence, by my mighty power and for the glory of my majesty?'" (Daniel 4:29,30). You hear, don't you, the faint echo of Satan's braggadocio to Christ when he spoke so vaingloriously of himself and the cosmic position he had assigned himself? "The devil led him up to a high place and showed him in an instant all the kingdoms of the world. And he said to him, 'I will give you all their authority and splendor, for it has been given to me, and I can give it to anyone I want to'" (Luke 4:5,6).

Like Satan's bold lie, Nebuchadnezzar's conceit warred against the First Commandment: "You shall have no other gods before me" (Exodus 20:3). Pride would lead men—including ministers—and angels to worship themselves instead of God.

Yes, one of the occupational hazards of the ministry is pride. Ministers occupy a high and lofty position. Say what you will about the erosion of respect the ministry has suffered in the public eye, the ministry still remains a uniquely influential element in American society. People who would automatically turn a deaf ear to policemen, judges, counselors, and psychiatrists will often still listen to their ministers. We ministers do hold a unique power over people. I

171

will always remember, for example, how a hardened criminal behaved while he was in the hands of the authorities. When questioned by the police, he denied his guilt and refused to tell the truth. But then when I saw him behind bars and reminded him of what God thought of his crimes, his demeanor turned meek, and I heard him admit to things he had refused to speak of with the authorities.

Because of the public positions we occupy and the personal power which we do hold over those who voluntarily submit themselves to our spiritual leadership, opportunities abound to invite our egos to climb up to the bar of self-aggrandizement or to grow resentful and pity ourselves when no one takes notice of the monuments which we have erected in honor of ourselves.

A minister must examine his motives when he experiences success and feels ambition driving him to seek even greater triumphs. Does he wish God to be glorified, or does he secretly hope to share a place with him in the worshipful spotlight? This is the "God-complex" with which Satan would tempt the successful minister even while he pursues outwardly defensible and beneficial parish goals. Oates says, "Another way you as a minister may substitute your relative authority for the sovereignty of God in the lives of your people is to use them as means for your own chosen ends rather than treating them as ends in themselves by reason of the fact that they are sacred human personalities 'for whom Christ died.' Thus you, the pastor, may let your function as administrator, builder of an organization, promoter of a budget, or leader of a crusade come into conflict with your representation of God. You must become a god yourself in order to manipulate your people toward your own predestined goal."[113]

To see how this might work out in our pastoral tasks let's run through this theoretical situation. Let's say you are faced with a major project or program in your parish. Your congregation wants to build a new church or establish an evangelism program or establish a parochial day school.

Here's where you come in. You enjoy your work in the congregation, and you get along well with the people. You and your people have built a solid relationship, and you see that things are progressing well. But you have a complaint. You feel that your people take you for granted. This feeling especially begins to gnaw at you as you set out to lay the groundwork for a parochial school.

Now, for years your parishioners have debated the merits of establishing such a school, but you mobilize your Church Council and propose that the idea of a school should at least receive some study.

With the formation of the study group the dream of a school gains substantive support. Momentum increases as the study group meets with representatives of other churches, visits other schools, and assembles cost figures. As your study group puts together a solid plan for the establishment of such a school, confidence begins to build among most of the members that they could accomplish something which has never been done before in their midst.

All the while you beat the drum to create a positive, up-beat attitude among the people, especially when some of the older people wonder out loud if the congregation can afford to enter into such a mammoth undertaking. Privately and publicly you use the power of your position to persuade and cajole the reluctant ones so that they are equal to the challenge of planting a school. You are elated to see the day when the church votes to go ahead with the plan.

Using your bulletins and church newsletters and sermons, you whip up enthusiasm to launch a fund drive. The congregation reacts positively and a sizable portion of the school's cost is collected before the first teacher arrives. You attend the opening service of the school with a great deal satisfaction, and as you see the children stream into their rooms, you could pop with joy.

Then as the joy and satisfaction of a job completed dims, you find yourself beset with mixed emotions. You hear your people, as the weeks and months go by, congratulating themselves for establishing such a wonderful school (program). You hear people say, "We should have done this years ago." But you fail to hear people give credit where you think some credit belongs—you hear only a few people say to you, "Good job, Pastor, we couldn't have done it without your leadership." You find yourself standing at a spiritual crossroads; one path leads to disenchantment and the other to dedication.

How many times in your ministry have you stood at such a juncture? You see the accomplishments of your time and talents. You behold the new building or the increase in church attendance or the smooth and efficient way your parish runs, *but* you feel cheated because your people are apparently failing to note that your talents and leadership played such an instrumental role. We may not set out consciously to build our successes to our glory, but in the course and pull of events we may have to admit to ourselves that we have managed to turn some of our successful projects into failed ego trips.

I recall a project I started in one of my churches that turned out far better than my wildest dreams. I gave this plan my all, and I was overjoyed to see how remarkably well it turned out. Yet when I saw how little recognition I received for it, I became depressed. But ultimately it dawned on me what had actually transpired. I had sold the people on the project's merit so well that they had made it their own; they had claimed ownership of it. As I reflected more on this development, I had to praise God for the way things worked out. God should be the one who winds up with the glory.

Take another example. John enjoyed the reputation of being a strong leader, capable preacher, and visionary. By encouraging, promoting, and explaining, John succeeded in convincing his parish that the time had arrived to replace their small and outdated school building with a bigger structure.

John threw his energies into the project with characteristic gusto, and he carried off the plan brilliantly. But in his efforts to marshal support he bullied some and upset others with his aggressive style of leadership. He paid the price, because after the congregation erected the building, some saw it as a monument to John's ego. The relationship between the pastor and his congregation soured, and John, upset with the congregation for their lack of gratitude for his leadership, left.

The God-complex which infected Nebuchadnezzar also searches out the ordinary, successful parish pastor, not merely the ministerial maniacs. Think of the God-complex as one of those common failings which should prompt a minister habitually to cry, "Who can discern his errors? Forgive my hidden faults" (Psalm 19:12).

I want to emphasize what I had said earlier: I have come to recognize my successes and abilities to be as dangerous as my failures and weaknesses. Success can go, as street talk puts it, to the head; personal triumphs can intoxicate, and they have a way of impairing judgment. It remains a devastating fact, for example, that David, at the height of his career, celebrated his military successes with his incredible act of adultery (2 Samuel 11:1-5). The conditions of our ministry are such that many ministers "are very aware of and like the attention and power of leadership."[114] Can any of us who stand in a pulpit afford to think that we are exempt from the temptation to grow proud when our tasks in ministry find visible and tangible success?

Giving God the Credit

God authors a minister's gifts, talents, and successes (James 1:17). God must consider it poor manners, therefore, for a man to see his successes, to hear compliments, and then to hoard the glory due someone else. Rather, make it a point to give God the glory.

Success can be the most wonderful experience if we appreciate it in its proper context. How good it makes us feel when our talents and energies succeed and when our motives have been aiming, from start to finish, to bring glory for God. I like the way Jay Adams puts it: "When we do everything for God's glory, then, whatever we do, we do in such a way that God's splendor shines through; he is given all the credit."[115] I like even better the way the Apostle Paul, in the following simple cause and effect statement, shows the relationship of a pastor's success in his duties to the goal of winning glory for God: "And they praised God because of me" (Galatians 1:24).

Summary

1. The object of ministerial success can spell doom for some pastors. Pride makes some men unable to stand success while it makes others intolerant of failure.
2. Success challenges ministers to remain humble. A successful minister may be tempted to want to act as God's replacement instead of his representative. Call this temptation the God-complex.
3. One of the minister's occupational "hazards" is growing proud. Parish pastors hold a unique power over people, and when they experience satisfactory results or great accomplishments, they may come to suffer from the "Nebuchadnezzar" syndrome—Nebuchadnezzar built Babylon for the "glory of [his] majesty." Ministers need to sort out their motivations in pursuing success. Are they seeking God's glory alone?

Advice

1. In descending order list the ten greatest successes in your ministerial career; however you wish to define the term success is up to you. After you have compiled your itemized list, reflect on how your successes affected your attitudes toward ministry. For example, if a successfully completed building project or book or home visitation headed your list, do some soul searching and ask some simple, basic questions: Did you get a "big head" out the experience? Did you feel cheated when you failed to win the recognition you felt you had coming? Did the experience leave you unchanged, or did you feel that something, good or bad, happened to you? Have you ever tried to discover what effect success has on you? What would your friends say success does to you? Your enemies?

2. Recheck your list of the ten greatest successes of your pastoral career. What success, currently missing from your list, would you dearly love to include? Why?

3. In descending order list your ten greatest fears of specific failure in ministry? How many of these fears have you personally experienced? How have they permanently affected your ministry?

Endnotes

[108] Richard Dortch, *Christianity Today* (18 March 1988): 47.

[109] See R. Robert Cueni, *What Ministers Can't Learn in Seminary* (Nashville: Abingdon Press, 1988), 121,122.

[110] *The Lutheran Hymnal* (St. Louis: Concordia Publishing House, 1941), 16.

[111] Wayne E. Oates, *The Christian Pastor* (Philadelphia: The Westminster Press, 1982), 72.

[112] Ibid., [Emphasis added].
[113] Ibid., 72,73.
[114] Rediger, *Coping with Clergy Burnout*, 40.
[115] Jay E. Adams, *Back to the Blackboard* (Phillipsburg, New Jersey: Presbyterian and Reformed Publishing Co., 1982), 22.

CHAPTER 11
HANDLING
THE HOLY IN
TIMELY
FASHION

Time Is a Bandit

Oh, they must have cut a smart picture!

Chapter 9 of Leviticus records the happy beginnings of the Aaronic priesthood in Israel. "Aaron and Sons" stepped into the light of that day in their spanking new robes to begin their worship tasks with excitement and dedication. Newly ordained, they handled the holy with success. God was pleased with their ministrations, and the people were moved to worship: "Fire came out from the presence of the LORD and consumed the burnt offering and the fat portions on the altar. And when all the people saw it, they shouted for joy and fell facedown" (Leviticus 9:24).

179

As you think back on the years you spent in preparation for the ministry, you can appreciate the scene and the emotions just described. On that ancient day theory and learning merged into practice and application. On that day Aaron and his sons were elated to be able to perform the duties and privileges God had entrusted to them.

There was a day like that for you—the day your classroom lectures and the required lot of tests, papers, and projects came to an end and gave way to an assignment which authorized you to apply your skills on behalf of God's people.

Stop for a moment and consider the forces at work when we humans enter on a new experience. What a fresh and exhilarating sensation the newness of a maiden voyage creates—whatever the passage. True, "every beginning is difficult," as an old German saw puts it. On the other hand, there's also nothing like the excitement of a beginning.

But the happy beginnings of the Aaronic priesthood crashed. How quickly, in fact, the whole situation turned tragic: "Aaron's sons Nadab and Abihu took their censers, put fire in them and added incense; and they offered unauthorized fire before the LORD, contrary to his command. So fire came out from the presence of the LORD and consumed them, and they died before the LORD" (Leviticus 10:1,2).

Speculation about the "unauthorized" work of Aaron's sons sees it as a deliberate act of unbelief on their part or as some sort of oversight. It fell to Moses to supply his brother Aaron with the commentary for what had happened to Nadab and Abihu. Moses said, "This is what the LORD spoke of when he said: 'Among those who approach me I will show myself holy; in the sight of all the people I will be honored.' Aaron remained silent" (Leviticus 10:3).

What causes ministers to be guilty of dishonoring God by botching or degrading ministerial assignments through second-rate efforts or half-hearted attempts?

Time, for one thing.

The passage of time, like a bandit, steals idealism, faithfulness, and conscientiousness. Other factors, which seek to rob us of the idealism with which we left seminary life, do, of course, exist. But the passage of time has the power to creep up without notice and to tarnish the glow on anyone's silver set of idealism.

Time Can Steal a Minister's Idealism

Do you remember the first time you pulled on your robes and entered the limelight of corporate worship as the preacher or liturgist? Can you recall some of the feelings that came over you when you stood as a novice before God's people? Did your knees shake? Did your mouth go dry? Did you experience a heightened sense of awareness? Were you especially conscious of the dignity of the moment and the utter seriousness of your ministration of God's Word?

I remember vividly my first such occasion, and I will share with you my impressions, because I hope to underscore how the passage of time has a deceptively slow but sure power to diminish one's idealism. Time changes one's perspective.

My first experience at a public ministration saw me motoring to a small Wisconsin town to assist the pastor with the liturgy and to help distribute Holy Communion. This happened in June, after I had completed my first year in the seminary, and I was fairly bursting with idealism. I had drunk deeply from the wisdom offered by my professors, and I was determined to do everything with the utmost awe and reverence.

When I reached that church and entered it through the sacristy door, only a last minute announcement that I was being teamed up with the church's janitor, garbed in clerical costume, to serve communion would have unnerved me more than the disappointment which assaulted my senses as I sized up the *pastor loci* (resident pastor). He welcomed my arrival and struck up a jovial conversation with me. I was shocked to hear him talk about his work in the off-hand manner I considered worthy of a chicken farmer describing the egg business; his blasé attitude seemed far from the ideal that I thought proper for a veteran of the ministry.

"He did everything wrong," I said to myself.

I stood there in the sacristy watching the man break every rule that I believed was held sacred by every acknowledged expert in ecclesiastical decorum. He handled nothing holy, I thought. And to top it off, he kept himself busy, before the communion service started, by smoking the minutes away. Not one cigarette. Three or four. I was horrified. I remembered one of my professors saying such a thing was never done before a service, as if it were unthinkable, but it was happening before my very eyes.

Twenty years have passed since my idealism was assaulted in my first ever ministerial experience. But I have nothing to crow about, as if I could boast that I have kept myself free from the tarnish of time. I must confess that over time my odyssey has also jaded my sensitivities.

I am going to tell you about an incident that happened to me but could just as well have happened to anyone else. In fact, you may have had a similar experience. My point in relating this incident is to have you consider how you might have reacted to this situation as a novice over against how you might react to it as a veteran of the ministry, grizzled by time.

It happened during a communion service—odd, how often the unusual strikes during this high moment in church life. And by this time in my life I had celebrated the sacrament countless times. I was standing at the altar with my back to the congregation, starring at the oaken Jesse Tree carving directly in front of me. I was participating with the people in the chanting of the Agnus Dei, and my mind was filled with holy thoughts. I had uncovered the chalice and the ciborium, and all was in readiness for the approach of the first communicants. Suddenly, out of nowhere, a horsefly shot past my nose with a buzz and hit the port in the chalice with a petite splash.

Just my luck, I told myself as I heaved a sigh.

Lutheran pastors come prepared for such emergencies, however, so I deftly picked up my gold-plated, perforated spoon, plunged it into the wine (the people are still singing the Agnus Dei), fished out the fly, and, with a flick of the wrist shot the invader against the sanctuary wall as neatly as if it had been catapulted off a carrier deck.

I remember being impressed with the aplomb I had handled this tricky situation, and all the more so that I had managed this feat under the watchful gaze of the worshipers without disturbing their worship. I also remember wondering what they would have thought if they had been able to see this little drama as it had unfolded before my eyes.

And yes, I served the wine to the people.

I told my wife about my little emergency. When she asked me whether I had served the wine to the people, I answered affirmatively, noting that "what they didn't know wouldn't hurt them."

My wife was horrified. She was very upset with me for doing something that I hadn't thought twice about under the circumstances

What would you have done? Would you have interrupted the service at that point and gone back to the sacristy to pour out the wine and start over again? My wife's startled reaction to my rather cavalier attitude got me to thinking about how much I had changed since my idealistic days as a novice. And I would have to admit that back in my twenty-second year of life, with only a year's worth of seminary training under my belt, I probably would have excused myself discreetly during the singing of an appropriate chant and with a holy disgust poured the contents of that cup down the drain.

My experience with the fly taught me, in some small way at least, that I had lost some of the wonderment of my holy calling over the course of time. Perhaps you have also learned this same truth about yourself through some experience that still remains fresh in your mind.

Time does many things to a minister. It becomes easy, as the years go by, to grow cynical and critical, hardened—if you know what I mean—no longer able to maintain the youthful idealism which marked one's outlook on the ministry at the outset.

I recall how Bob, a seminary student, liked to engage me in friendly debate about my approach to ministry. He maintained that he would do things quite differently if he were in my shoes. I enjoyed Bob's idealism and felt a kinship of sorts with him. I just loved to listen to him talk, because in his conversation I could hear myself, as a seminary student, talking, cocksure that I had all the answers; his words filled me with nostalgia for a time in my life that had come and gone.

After Bob entered the ministry, he set about putting into practice the idealistic strategies he had amassed in the seminary; I felt good for him, in that he was being true to his convictions. After he had spent a couple of years in his first parish, I had an occasion to ask him how things were faring. I had to chuckle at his answer. He told me that he had gone about his work aggressively, and, knowing Bob's boundless energies, I have no doubt that he really set his congregation on fire in his idealistic attempt to solve all of its problems in short order. Unfortunately, Bob's aggressiveness prompted more than one parishioner to send him away with a flea in his ear, and I felt sorry for him as he related to me his disappointments.

"Where is all the idealism you used to have?" I asked Bob.

Bob puffed out his cheeks and then—to express his disgust—expelled a long, noisy gush of air. "Idealism? It's gone." And he laughed one of those laughs that says, "I'm really exaggerating, but I am disappointed at how things have turned out."

Bob's exaggerated disappointment about his lost idealism also surfaces in the pastoral conferences that I attend, where with increasing frequency pastors find a ready audience to air their complaints and criticisms of the ministry. And I have to confess that I, too, have used these occasions to voice some negative attitudes.

Repetition Can Be the Mother of Incompetence

Familiarity breeds contempt.

You buy a new car and wash it every Saturday morning. Four years later it has rusted and collected dents. Then you wash it only when it absolutely needs it. Yes, familiarity breeds contempt.

The passage of time makes a minister thoroughly familiar with all his tasks and duties. As a result he can develop a rather flippant or nonchalant attitude toward those "jobs" he finds himself doing over and over again. They begin to loose that certain edge. They no longer are special, and, thus, he begins to treat them with disrespect.

Think of your parishioners. You observe them month after month, and even as they grow to recognize your habits and idiosyncrasies, so you also become adept at diagnosing their weaknesses, tendencies, and characteristics. As a certain familiarity sets in, that special way of treating your parishioners, with which you began your ministry to them, begins to fade. You may even be tempted at times to treat them contemptuously. And then you get into trouble.

Think also of all your specific tasks and assignments. Endlessly (or so it would seem) repeating the same tasks—turning out newsletters, bulletins, and congregational letters, preaching and teaching, making calls, and attending meetings—may tempt us to do just enough to slide by.

Yes, repetition may be the mother of incompetence.

Handling the Holy with Callused Hands

The sad tale of Nadab and Abihu, Aaron's son's whose "unauthorized" fire displeased God, underscores the need for God's ministers to treat their public ministrations with the utmost respect and dignity. God's glory demands it. "Among those who approach me I will show myself holy; in the sight of all the people I will be honored" (Leviticus 10:3).

I have no quarrel with the spirit of God's directive. God's ministrations require a reverent attitude. But I also wonder if it is possible to take the matter of reverence to an extreme. In the first division of this chapter I discussed how time can tarnish the special way in which we handle our pastoral duties, thus resulting in sloppy work. But can the reverse also happen? Might the passing years see a minister's work travel in the very opposite direction, becoming so rigid and mechanically correct that his people draw the conclusion that he carries out his work under a threat from God to do it right or die? And the people wonder, "What happened to our pastor's sensitivities? Did he build up some calluses over the years?"

Those Strict Disciples

Just as Nadab and Abihu's irreverence went to one extreme in their use of "unauthorized fire," the disciples of Jesus, I submit, went to the opposite extreme when they reacted so fiercely to the interruption caused by those mothers who brought babies to Jesus for his blessings. The disciples attempted to shoo them away and prevent them from interrupting Jesus while he was instructing the crowds on the important issues related to marriage and divorce. Jesus reacted to his disciples' behavior in an equally fierce manner: "People were bringing little children to Jesus to have him touch them, but the disciples rebuked them. When Jesus saw this, he was indignant" (Mark 10:13,14). Jesus had no use for the strictness which marked the disciples' reaction to the interruption posed by the mothers with their babies.

I find it significant that this incident took place, not during the disciple's novitiate days, but in the final days of Christ's ministry. The disciples who bawled out the mothers were veteran disciples, schooled disciples, disciples experienced in the circumstances attendant to the public ministry of the Lord. Moreover, they were disciples who were zealous for the work of the Lord. They would tolerate no breach of public etiquette when it came to their Lord and his Word. But from our Lord's response we also understand that their zeal had crossed over the middle ground that exists between reverence and lovelessness.

I see the strictness that marked the behavior of the veteran apostles as the more likely problem to beset the veteran minister who seeks to handle the holy things of God with reverence and awe.

When I Shooed Away the Babies

One Sunday I found myself in a situation that tested my sensitivities to the task of handling the holy things of God with an even hand. In fact, I found myself on familiar ground with the disciples: how would I react when someone threatened to disrupt a service where people were giving their attention to God's Word.

You must first appreciate the circumstances under which I passed through this fiery trial. I was conducting a German language service for about thirty people who were scattered about in the cavernous expanse of the church. I was in the pulpit. I had just begun to read my sermon (important point—I was forced to preach looking down because of my inability to memorize six pages of a German sermon), when suddenly I spied a form to my left at the outer limits of my peripheral vision. The usher had opened the door directly to the left of my pulpit, you see, since it was a hot, August day.

As I continued to read my sermon, I began to notice some movement from the form. My interest piqued. To satisfy my curiosity I snuck a glance at the shapeless form. I found that I was being spied upon by a young boy who wore shorts and an oversized pair of sunglasses in a hideous shade of pink. What was he up to? I asked myself.

I was determined to ignore him. My dignity and that of the service, I believed, was at stake. The lad, however, took my snub as a challenge. Before I finished reading page three, I noticed that he was standing on the threshold of the open door. Nevertheless, on I read.

After what seemed like hours, I came to the next page. I'm only on page four? Two more to go! I groaned inwardly. By then the boy had moved again. He's inside the church, I noted to myself as the kid took a couple of steps toward me and planted himself beside the oak stand which held the hymn numbers. I noticed a stirring in the crowd of Germans. They now knew what I knew. I felt myself frozen with indecision. What should I do now? Still refusing to acknowledge the boy's presence, I read on, knowing full well that none of my listeners was paying attention to a word I was reading.

Page five, I'm on page five now, only one more to go, I said to myself. And I noticed with relief that the boy was not moving. Good, I thought. Just make him stay there, dear God, until I get through.

I will never forget with what relief I spoke that Amen. I had maintained my dignity and that of the church I loved. One duty remained before I could turn, leave the pulpit, and fasten a glare on the boy that would melt him. I still had to pray the Lord's Prayer.

I was only halfway through the prayer when I saw the boy begin to move again. He had left his post beside the hymn numbers and was now climbing the stairs up to my pulpit. I prayed as Jesus had never taught his disciples to pray. "Amen," I said, and I whirled to square off with my tormentor.

"Nicholas!"

The three-year-old boy with the hideous pink sunglasses was none other than my youngest boy. I was mortified.

Nicholas stood on the second step and beamed at me through his pink sunglasses. All I could think of was to point to the open door. "Go!" I ordered, and as a centurion had once reported to Jesus of his men's willingness to carry out his orders, so I could say that my son went.

I entered my sacristy, sensing the scandal that would result from this incident. I could already hear the comments that my children lacked discipline. I could envision getting phone calls from outraged parishioners announcing that they would take their membership elsewhere, where the pastor's kids would not turn the service into a joke. I was so shook up and embarrassed that I could barely think, but in those few minutes I managed to fashion together a hastily worded apology.

Before I turned to the altar to pray, I apologized to the people (in English) for my son's actions, and I added a thought which I figured would pull some of my reputation back out of the fire, "And I promise you that he will never do anything like this again." I figured that this promise to restore order to my family and to the decorum of the worship service would endear me to the group.

When I turned to pray, I had no idea that none of the people had it in mind to join me in my holy thoughts, or that my words had only succeeded in moving them to enter into a massive conspiracy against me behind my back. For, when I went to the doors to greet the thirty worshipers—

wouldn't you know it—I was the one in trouble, not my boy.

I knew instinctively that I was in trouble the moment I saw Frau Fleischmann make a beeline for me. Usually one of the slowest ones down the steps to the main doors of the church, she had somehow managed to sprout wings and was the first to arrive. By the look on her face I knew she meant to scold me. This stern old woman, this survivor of the Bolshevik revolution, this woman who used to greet my visits to her apartment with the snide greeting, "Vell, who have you t'rown out of the church now," this ninety-eight pounds of intimidation hobbled up to me, shaking a bony finger at me—like a dying wasp intent on plunging its barb one last time into its victim—and croaked out a stinging warning: "Don't you lay vun hand on dat boy, Herr Pastor. You should be t'ankful that he vants to come to church und be mit his fat'er. You von't raise your hand to schtrike him!"

That was the first and worst of the chiding I received that morning from this ordinarily stern and very reserved group of Germans. I could not believe it. I had attempted to discipline myself to keep the service from breaking down. I had concentrated on doing what I believed had to be done. But I had read the group wrong, and my corrective actions completely backfired.

What lessons would you draw from my experience? I am still trying to figure them out, but I will give you one major impression it left on me. I think the thing I lacked, the thing that was so apparently missing and thus drew such a reaction from my thirty listeners—in that holy but disrupted moment of public worship—was love. "Dad" wanted to execute the service as it had been written, as we Lutherans like to put it, "in a fitting and orderly way" (1 Corinthians 14:40). But all that I managed to do through my behavior was to show the people that I was a mean guy.

What would I do differently if I had to do it all over again? Knowing what I know now, I would smile a little smile, pat my Nicholas on the head, take him into the sacristy, not say a word to him until we both were out of sight of the worshipers, and then have a talk with him about church decorum later. You know, I don't remember a thing about that sermon I preached that day, and my thirty listeners don't either, but unfortunately they remember something else I showed them. If we are going to preach a message of love, I suppose we had better send out the right signals as we do it. Right?

Life presents us with its choice of extremes, does it not? In our efforts to handle the holy with holy hands, may we strive for that evangelical middle ground that lies between the actions of the sons of Aaron, who displeased God because of their lack of reverence, and the actions of the disciples of Jesus, who displeased him because of their strictness. Time can steal our reverence, but it can also turn us into callused veterans and make us insensitive and ungracious individuals. The glory of God is his grace; may the years never tarnish our reflection of it.

Tender Hands

Otto A. Geiseman, sainted pastor of historic Grace Lutheran Church in River Forest, Illinois, wonderfully caught and expressed the meaning of what a glorious, gracious privilege it is to serve as a minister of God: "We must be persons who have been taken in hand by the Spirit of God and led to the top of Mount Calvary. We must be persons to whom the divine Spirit has explained who this One is that hangs on the center cross. We must be persons who, each individually, have known the joy of finding Christ as our personal Savior and of shouting triumphantly to all the world: 'That is my Lord, who has redeemed me, a lost and condemned creature.'"[116]

191

Competency—refusing to give up, working like a shepherd, guarding against pride, emulating Christ's spirit of humility, and managing well the major and minor tasks of ministry—is a matter of vision. While the passage of time tends to jade his perspective, the minister can, as Geiseman wisely advises, always refocus his vision by returning to what Luther called the theologia crucis (the theology of the cross).

The sight of God's Son, suspended for sinners on the cross, represents the apex of God's glory—his grace. That sight defines the term gospel. Michael Horton, editor of *The Agony of Deceit*, a volume that exposes the heresies of many of TV's famous preachers, gets at the heart of what makes the cross such good news for sinners, when he writes, "The gospel was never intended to show people how to save themselves with God's help. The law was designed to drive them to despair of saving themselves so that they would give up their self-improvement struggle for salvation and cast themselves entirely on God's mercy. Jesus did not come to make people redeemable, but to actually purchase those who were wicked, alienated, and hostile to that redemption. He does not 'help those who help themselves,' but saves those who are entirely helpless to lift a finger."[117]

Exactly! The cross of Jesus shines as God's greatest glory—his unmerited mercy, his grace. Let us who proclaim its message, likewise, find in it a constant source of personal inspiration and strength, together with the desire to handle our holy tasks with the even hand of reverence and sensitivity.

The sight of the God-in-the-flesh on Golgotha's cross makes us remember our sinfulness and our need humbly to acknowledge our guilt and culpability before God. To cultivate such a spirit of humility will not shatter, but actually encourage competency. On this matter Geiseman says, "If we pastors are humbly aware of our sins and are sincerely ashamed of them, it will also be easier for us honestly and readily to admit when we have made mistakes of judgment, misbehaved, or failed in some other way."[118]

To catch sight of God's glory in the crucified Christ makes and keeps a person humble, receptive, and tender in spirit. I am, for example, sensitive to criticisms just as I would suppose you are. I count it no great joy ride to be the recipient of criticism. Much less do I seek it out. And yet criticism does facilitate competency when it confronts us with those faults that build up in the course of time just like calluses on our hands and when we then take that criticism to heart and make amends.

Accordingly, handling the holy in a timely fashion may mean humbling ourselves to seek out and welcome professional criticism, as painful as that may be, as well as readily accepting the unsolicited corrections which our friends and parishioners give us periodically. The passage of time has a sneaky way of making a man inattentive or unaware, or making a man comfortable with his poor attitudes and work habits. Time may also see us insulating ourselves from constructive criticisms by means of sophisticated rationalizations about our shortcomings.

Dan had a reputation as a good preacher. Dan knew that God had blessed him in this regard, and he worked hard in developing his sermon preparation and delivery. When Dan was asked to preach at his local pastors' conference, he was honored, and his brothers received his message enthusiastically.

Then Mike stood up to comment on Dan's message, and while he, too, complimented Dan on the substance of his sermon, he offered some constructive criticism. He noted that Dan spoke too fast. Mike also pointed out that Dan failed to pause sufficiently after the effective illustrations he had used and that, as a result, their meaning did not sink in. Dan's sermon delivery, in short, still needed work.

Dan didn't remember many of the glowing compliments he had received that day; Mike's criticism crowded out all the pleasant things he had heard. Dan sulked for a few days thereafter, trying to justify his rapid-fire delivery, but after some reflection Dan had to admit that Mike was right.

It took some time, but Dan corrected this problem which had developed over the course of preaching hundreds of sermons. He slowed his delivery. And when he used illustrations, Dan would type the word PAUSE in bold caps after those illustrations which he considered especially good.

Time dulls sensitivities. Time builds calluses on our sensitivities through repetitive acts. So we need the objective critiques of people who love us. Scripture says, "Better is open rebuke than hidden love. The kisses of an enemy may be profuse, but faithful are the wounds of a friend" (Proverbs 27:5,6).

Let then the glorious picture of the cross, God's grace in action, fill us with whatever humbleness we need in order to refocus our attitudes. If God could stoop to save and to serve sinners, cannot we, who serve, stoop in order to learn better how to serve God and sinners in timely fashion?

Do It for God

No right thinking minister of God wants to duplicate the sin of Nadab and Abihu by doing something "unauthorized" (Leviticus 10:1). Therefore, I have suggested one way to experience a heightened sense of dedication and to cultivate the desire to make professional improvements: through a spirit of humility.

A second way to preserve in us a timely sense of reverence and sensitivity towards the holy tasks of ministry? Try worship.

Worship?

Who of us, when we were children, did not ask our mothers, "Is that all we're going to do in heaven, sing songs?" You may have phrased your question somewhat differently than I did, but one way or another the thought apparently impressed us all in our youth that there was something inherently boring about worship. But the truth is that worship is exciting!

And worship energizes competency.

To prove the accuracy of my claim that worship is exciting and that it energizes competency, I invite you to participate in this little experiment. Let's see how it plays out.

First, at what time of the year do you happen to be reading this volume? Is it around Christmas? Easter? For the sake of our experiment let's assume that it's close to Christmas. (If it's closer to Easter or Thanksgiving or some other high festival, please feel free to substitute your closest holiday.)

So let's say that Christmas has come. You are tired and worn out. You have spent many hours preparing Christmas for others. Now the hour has come for the service, and you survey the scene. What you see and smell differs in no way from last year's holiday service. The air hangs heavy with a mustiness that only an interior, filled with people in every available space, can create. Despite the regulations set down by the local fire department, your ushers have set up folding chairs in the aisles for the latecomers. As you look out over the people, you feel your adrenaline pumping, for the moment of worship beckons. You wear a smile on your face. The stage is set.

Whoever said worship was boring? By the time the service is finished, you feel a golden glow emanating from the people and yourself. You have seen the glory of God. You have tasted once again the goodness of his grace. You have drunk the joys of salvation. You have felt communion with God and heaven. And as you bask in the preciousness of that high point of worship, never would you, even for a moment, consider becoming a lazy, irresponsible bum in Christ.

To the contrary, your worship experience has re-energized your sense of dedication. I have felt that way in and after the great moments of worship, and so have you. We all have found ourselves swept away by the power of worship, worship in which our words and actions of praise laid hold of their object, God, to give him the glory. And in return we felt a measure of satisfaction and happiness. And as those great realities nestled in our souls—as we heard the last hymn of the service sung, or as we spoke a benediction over the people, or as we shook the hands of the worshipers at the doors—we told ourselves, "I want to do it again, I want to do it better." And I have a sneaking suspicion—or, at least, so I have been told—that some of you were so re-energized by your newly found rededication and reverence derived from your worship experience that you could not restrain yourselves, but that you had to sit down immediately after the service to begin writing next year's Christmas sermon.

Worship does that. It inspires, and it rededicates.

Would that we could bottle the inspiration of seeing God's glory so that we could pour it out on ourselves in liberal doses when we find our hands growing weary, when, like Moses at the battle of Rephidim (Exodus 17:8-13), we want to drop them to our sides and give up the crusade of ministry.

I can provide you with no easy formulas whereby you can reduce the glory of God to some sort of an elixir or tonic, nor am I suggesting that we pursue the glorification of God as an end in itself so that we can manipulate worship as some self-serving therapy to pump new life into our careers. No, we give the glory to God for what he has done for us out of his grace and mercy; he has made and saved us. But as we worship him, the experience will leave us affected indirectly, even as it aimed to affect God directly by pleasing him through faith. My point is that, as we deliberately remind ourselves that all our pastoral acts, and not just the highly emotional ones like Christmas and Easter services, constitute acts of glorification which God finds pleasure in, we just may find ourselves saying, I want to do it again; I want to do it better.

All hangs on our deliberately entering into all of our ministerial actions with the thought, I am worshiping God. When we conduct a Christmas service, we do not have to force ourselves to see it as an act of worship, for that fact stands apparent. But, do we perform all the other tasks of ministry with the same perspective all of the time? Do we pursue them as a matter of routine, or do we consciously set about to worship God in and through them?

This is what I meant back at the end of Chapter 1, when I made the unsupported claim that to the degree that you know how God is glorified in your pastoral ministrations and to the extent you consciously minister with God's glorification as your only goal, you will experience (among other things) a heightened sense of dedication.

Can't you see it? As you go trudging up the stairs of the hospital to visit a sick parishioner, you can have a number of motivations in mind for doing what you are about to do.

You can think, "I *have* to do this because I'm getting paid to do this." Bad.

You can think, "I *want* to do this because the person is in trouble, and the person needs my help and support." Good.

You can think, "I *want* to make this call because the person needs my help and support, and I hope that I will be of help and support, but whatever happens, I know that my faithful actions will bring glory to God." Best.

Train yourself to think this way. The more you consciously and deliberately go about your ministrations, knowing that your faithful efforts work the glorification of God, the more you will sense a growing dedication that says, I want to do it again, I want to do it better.

Catch the glorious vision of Christ and make competency a holy crusade, combining your small and ordinary, repetitious tasks together with your *Christmas* and *Easter* ones into daily cathedrals of worship to the glory of God.

Summary

1. The passage of time, much like a bandit, steals from ministers their sense of idealism and their sense of reverence for their pastoral acts. The repetitive acts of ministry can create boredom.
2. The passage of time also can make ministers insensitive or callused towards those whom they serve. This can come about when ministers are more concerned with protocol than the spirit of the gospel. Those who preach the message of God's love need to strive for the middle ground between strictness and sensitivity, so that they avoid coming across to their parishioners as mean or legalistic.
3. Humility encourages the desire to be aware of the faults which you as a minister may collect over the course of time.
4. Worship encourages the desire to rededicate one's self to ministerial tasks, to do them better and better. The challenge for the minister is to see every pastoral act as a form of worship and to deliberately remind himself of that fact as he enters into each pastoral act.

Advice

1. Professionals of many different types use workshops, seminars, and degree programs to upgrade their skills. If you have been out of the seminary for more than ten years, consider some type of disciplined course of study to improve your preaching or teaching or counseling techniques. Especially consider courses of study in those areas where you know you have problems to correct.

2. If you resist the idea of taking self-improvement programs, how about settling for a self-help study? Just about everyone has a camcorder. Rent one or borrow one, if you do not own one, and have someone videotape your preaching or teaching. Perhaps you do not relish the idea of seeing what the tape would reveal, but I guarantee that if you were to develop a personal library of live recordings of your preaching or teaching activities, you would quickly spot things you would want to correct.

3. The pastoral conference which I attend used to feature a sermon and service critique in which the ministers offered constructive criticism of each other's preaching and liturgical practices. The critiquing was discontinued when some of the ministers found it too threatening, but I found it the most stimulating and practical element of these meetings. You might want to consider meeting periodically with neighboring pastors for mutual help (Proverbs 25:5,6).

Endnotes

[116] Richard R. Caemerer, Otto A. Geiseman et al., *The Pastor at Work* (St. Louis: Concordia Publishing House, 1960), 17.

[117] Michael Horton, ed., *The Agony of Deceit* (Chicago: Moody Press, 1990), 139 [Emphasis added].

[118] Caemerer, Geiseman et al., *The Pastor at Work*, 17.

CHAPTER 12
THE IMPORTANCE OF PRAYER AND MEDITATION

The Need for Personal Devotions Is Great

As a seminary student, I heard or read statements that disturbed me. None struck me more than one by Veit Dietrich about Martin Luther's prayer habits during those harrowing days of 1530 when Charles V was presiding at the Diet of Augsburg to determine the fate of Lutheranism. Dietrich reported to Melanchthon in a letter that, while Luther awaited its outcome in a castle in Coburg, "Not a day passes during which he [Luther] does not spend in prayer at least three hours, such as are most precious for study."[119]

How could anyone spend that much time in prayer when there was so much to do, I wondered. I could not imagine even Jesus spending three hours a day in prayer.

In the previous chapter, I made the statement that time changes a person's perspectives. Time also adds a mass of concerns to a man's life, concerns that cause him to have more to pray for as he grows older. When I was a student in the seminary, I remember praying most frequently and urgently, and almost solely, for a wife. Since my graduation God has blessed me with a wonderful wife and family and a ministry. He has also given me many, many more concerns than occupied my mind while I was a seminary student. Consequently, I find my prayer agenda resembling my wife's recipe box—so filled with precious thoughts (none of which I can bear to discard), that I can no longer close the lid on them. Would that I had Luther's stamina and self-discipline to spend at least an hour a day in giving my concerns their prayerful due.

My inability to pray in the style of Luther, however, does not minimize my conviction that a strong prayer life contributes mightily to our prime directive of glorifying God in our ministerial acts. To the contrary, the busier the pastor becomes, the more he will need to pray; the busier a pastor becomes, the more he grows dependent on Christ and his counsel to keep his vision of soli Deo gloria clear.

Christ is the Minister's Pastor

I find it ironic to note the disparity between the ways my spiritual needs are met over against the ways my parishioners' needs are satisfied. My people have me to shepherd them with the Word of the chief Shepherd. To whom can I look for pastoral help?

Yes, to whom can the pastor look for pastoral help?

I put this question to a group of ministers from different Protestant denominations, and their answers are interesting.

Here are some of them:

"Theory: District Superintendent. Practice: none."[120]

"My associate and my day school principal."[121]

"Good question—I don't have one. I guess a close friend who is also a pastor."[122]

"My wife, who is also my best friend."[123]

"I have two or three. My district President is an effective pastor to pastors. I also have a neighboring pastor I confide in, and a non-pastor neighbor who is a very trusted friend."[124]

"My district Superintendent."[125]

"I talk with my bishop, but my pastor is a colleague in the United Church of Christ. Theologically we are different, but his faith and warmth are very real."[126]

In general, most ministers told me that for pastoral help they turned to their denominational supervisors (superintendent, bishop, coalition chairman). Second place honors went to wives! Denominational colleagues, neighboring pastors, and friends, in that order, rounded out their personal choices. Two ministers had no answers.[127]

I found most insightful the answer that came from a pastor in the Lutheran Church—Missouri Synod, who wrote, "Basically, the Lord Jesus Christ [is my pastor]. I find that fellow clergymen do not always have or care to take time to listen to concerns of a brother in the Lord." (I was surprised that Christ was listed only three times as the minister's pastor and, then, only in combination with others.)[128]

I side with the Missouri Synod pastor, who saw Christ as his pastor, but my reason for doing so is different. Christ is my pastor, not by default (I can find no one else), but because of his abilities (whom better can I find). We ministers serve under the Great Shepherd; we should see Christ as the one best qualified to shepherd our souls. To whom should the shepherd under Christ turn to, look to, and appeal to, as his pastor, other than the one who said, "Come to me, all you who are weary and burdened, and I will give you rest. Take my yoke upon you and learn from me, for I am gentle and humble in heart, and you will find rest for your souls "(Matthew 11:28,29).

This "Shepherd and Overseer" (1 Peter 2:25) of souls ministers through his Word and Sacraments. He answers the prayers of his ministers. He pastors the pastors; not only is he is equipped to do so, but he is also willing to help. In fact, only in Christ does the minister have a pastor who is perfectly able to help him.

When the pastor faces baffling problems, when he is painfully aware of his own inadequacy, when he is overwhelmed by the vastness of the responsibility that has been entrusted to him, he always needs to remember that, not only does he have the privilege of casting his concerns and cares *upon the Lord* (1 Peter 5:7), but also that all of the resources of his wise and powerful heavenly Father have been placed at his disposal in the promise that his prayer will be heard and answered. Great men of God like St. Paul and Luther were made what they were partly through their intense use of prayer and the *Lord's answer* to their prayer.[129]

The Sacra Privata Keeps the Vision Clear

Jay Adams underscores a valid truth when he says that better preaching and teaching results when a pastor cultivates and sustains "a vital relationship with God."[130] Adams writes, "While fixing the shoes of others, the shoemaker's own soles may wear through. Physician heal yourself! It is so easy for the minister, in spite of Paul's warning (1 Timothy 4:14-16), in becoming a servant to the flock, to neglect himself. This may be remedied by continually remembering that he must glorify God."[131]

How does the servant to the flock continually remember that he must glorify God? He must take refuge in his own *sacra privata* (private holy time) wherein he daily confronts himself with the Christo-centric emphasis of the Scriptures, sensitizes himself anew to the grace of God, and experiences the reality of the love of God for him, an unworthy human being. A textbook from the turn of the century, *The Lutheran Pastor*, gives this worthwhile advise: "The true soul-winners and soul-feeders have always felt their own utter insufficiency. They have been men of prayer; they have realized the need of regular closet hours; they have been much alone with God; they have constantly found refreshment, strength, peace, and joy in their still hours. Their inner, devotional life has had its daily attention, nourishment, and furtherance. They have always been busy men, but they always had a regular time for their own *sacra privata*."[132]

This same textbook also warns ministers against the danger of neglecting their souls: "Surely his [the minister's] is a great work, a responsible work, a work fraught with tremendous possibilities and consequences. Who is sufficient for these things? No one in his own strength. God pity the pastor who depends on his own wisdom, wit, or tact for all this."[133] I have imagined myself the object of such pity. It is so easy to neglect one's own sacra privata and argue, "I have too many things to do, or I am too tired."

And aren't those just the times—when the sight of God's glorious grace hides behind the clouds—that there is a tendency to focus on the frustrations of ministry, to have the feeling that you are facing two hours worth of road work with only one hour's worth of gas in the tank? The ring of the phone, the buzzing of the doorbell, the unscheduled drop-in visitor—they all seem to upset me the most on those days that see me spending the least amount of time with my heavenly Pastor (that is, having a two-way conversation with him, where you hear what he says, and you respond). Reading what God has to say (Scripture) is no substitute (I say this at the risk of being misunderstood) for the necessity of telling God what we have on our minds (prayer). God wants us to hear what he has to tell us, but he also commands us to tell him what we have to say (John 16:24; Ephesians 6:18; 1 Thessalonians 5:17). Your role and mine, as pastors, must be seen in that context—we talk with people, and they talk to us. Why should we imagine that our Lord's role as our Pastor is to be any different from that which exists between us and our people.

Even when our ministries sap us of our strength and wear us down, the Overseer (1 Peter 2:25) of our souls stands ready to hear us and help us. It amazes me how differently I look at things after I have spent time in prayer with my Pastor. My vision is restored. My confidence returns. My strength is renewed. You would think that after such experiences I would want to spend more and more time in prayer, and I do. But sadly I also find it the most difficult activity of my ministry to keep at. Even though I have witnessed how God has answered my prayers with thundering accuracy, and I could almost smell the smoke (1 Kings 18:36-38), prayer continues to remain a struggle.

Forces That Work against Prayer

Jacob wrestled with God in the night till daybreak at Peniel (Genesis 32:24). It cost him; it left him with a new name and a limp. How quickly do you think Jacob would have wanted a rematch? Prayer is a wrestling. Martin E. Lehman, writing in his *Luther and Prayer*, quotes the early church fathers on this point: "There is no labor so hard as prayer."[134]

A Little Survey Work on Prayer Time

Prayer takes work. That probably explains why few people spend more than a few minutes a day doing it. I put this question to one of my confirmation classes: How much time do you spend in prayer each day? To insure the honesty and accuracy of their answers, I allowed the children to submit their responses unsigned.

Thirty seconds! The average time spent by the seventh and eighth graders of my confirmation class amounted to thirty seconds per day.

I then asked nineteen seasoned veterans of the ministry, "How much time do you spend each day in personal prayer and meditation?" The answers ranged from twenty minutes to one hour a day. The average time was thirty-six minutes. I regret, however, phrasing my question as I did. I have no way of telling how much time each man spent in petitionary and intercessory prayer as opposed to Bible reading. I would guess that actual prayer time lagged behind Bible reading—reading is simply easier to do. The only way I can confirm my theory is to request that you examine your prayer habits. How much time do you spend in prayer each day? Excluding Bible reading, how much actual time do you give yourself for petitionary and intercessory prayer? Thirty minutes? Ten minutes? Five minutes? Or thirty seconds?

Beliefs about the Average Pastor

If you are like me, an average pastor, you do not pray enough. Now, you can write me a letter telling me that I am wrong, but chances are that you will fail to move me. I know how I have handled prayer throughout my life, and I also know that my approach to prayer differs little from my classmates and colleagues in the ministry. Everything I have seen and heard and read tells me that the average minister fails to prayer "continually" (1 Thessalonians 5:17).

Why? As I said previously, it takes work to pray. Luther himself said that when he approached his *sacra privata* he was forced to design ways to get himself in the proper mood; he called this preparatory time a "warming up" for prayer, a time in which he played his lute or sang songs. Even the great Reformer did not automatically find prayer easy.

Do the words, "it takes work to pray," suggest then that some of us who fail to pray as we should are lazy? I do so confess.

But that diagnosis fails to give us a full explanation of why some of us are neglecting to give as much time as we should to prayer.

Some of us just apparently refuse to believe that prayer is as important as Scripture makes it. And we have all our little arguments in place to justify our lack of wrestling with God.

Some of us fail to pray continually, strangely enough, because of our high view of Scripture. Somehow we have gotten the idea that if we take twenty minutes to read two or three chapters of God's Word—which takes less work than praying twenty minutes—then we can afford to forgo or minimize the process of responding to God in prayer. We tell ourselves that since the Holy Spirit uses his Word to plant and maintain faith and since prayer fails to qualify as a means of grace, prayer is less important than Bible reading.

Some of us approach the Scripture and hear God speak to us in his perfect Word. Then, having heard the Word, we close our Bibles, tap our heads with it, let loose a long exegetical "Ahhhhhhh," and thinking that we have done all the meditating that is necessary, conclude, "Now it's time for action. Now we can get to work." But only after we have taken that Word and also tapped our *hearts* with it and prayed to God about it, can we sit back and exclaim, "Ahaaaaaaa!" Then do we have it. Only then are we ready to get to work.

I know well the mentality that makes it possible to make prayer a stepchild to exegesis, for I have done exactly that myself. Let me draw the scene for you. The pastor faces a task. The task is right up his alley, an assignment that involves scriptural research and putting the results of that research down on paper. This task allows him to put into practice the vast array of skills with which his undergraduate and seminary training has equipped him. He approaches his assignment with the craft and skill of a technocrat, wringing every possible bit of information from his research into Scripture.

This man's assignment can be a sermon, the latest stewardship strategy, or a Bible class study. He works for five or ten or a hundred hours to achieve his goal. But how much unnecessary work may he have put in, if he has neglected to take the necessary step of first taking the matter up with God in prayer and then continuing to pray the project through? So too, when we spend twenty hours on an assignment but have only used thirty seconds of that time in prayer for its success, why should we be surprised when the results of our work leave us disappointed?

Some of us fail to pray continually because we have come to think that it is the confessional thing to do. Some of us act as if a greater emphasis on the amount of time one should expend in prayer was created by Pietists or the sacramentally poor as a plot to draw the unsuspecting child of heaven away from Word and Sacrament. Never mind, of course, that while Lutheranism hung in the balance in 1530, Martin Luther was spending three hours a day praying.

Some of us fail to pray continually because we overreact to the excesses of those who have devalued the sacraments and have given the impression that they have substituted prayer in their place. In seeking to avoid this extreme we go to the other extreme and neglect prayer.

Some of us fail to pray continually because our study of God's Word and the high view we bring to it causes us to intellectualize our approach to matters spiritual. Let the lay people pray, this mentality says, we pastors will do the thinking. This intellectualizing of spirituality, I submit, constitutes the one great downside to the *grammatico-historical* approach to Scripture. I believe in this approach to Scripture, but I also know that—perhaps, as a result—I am curiously tempted to treat the Bible as the chief textbook from which dogma is drawn rather than as God's living Word whose purpose it is to draw me into a personal relationship with him. F. LaGard Smith in *Fallen Shepherds Scattered Sheep* looks at this phenomenon from the standpoint of his training as a lawyer. He notes that there are lawyers who know the fine points of the law but lack sensitivity in using it. He compares this tendency to that of biblical scholars who may know the Bible backwards and forwards, but who fail to have a personal relationship with God because they have amassed only academic knowledge.[135]

An active prayer life balances an intense, exegetical life, preventing a theologically conservative pastor from turning into a religious technocrat. This balance, I theorize, made Luther the practical and powerful pastor and professor he was, as much at home on his knees in prayer as he was on his chair in the study of Scripture.

Whatever the hang-ups and the forces which seek to short circuit your prayer time with God, Jesus urges you to set them aside. He wants to hear from you on a regular basis. Jesus told the parable of the persistent widow to show his disciples "that they should always pray and not give up (Luke 18:1). And Paul says, "And pray in the Spirit on all occasions with all kinds of prayers and requests. With this in mind, be alert and always keep on praying for all the saints" (Ephesians 6:18).

Jesus also wants to answer your requests. That we fail to pray "on all occasions with all kinds of prayers and requests" explains why perhaps we lack so many things and fail to see results. "You do not have, because you do not ask God" (James 4:2).

And I would ask you to consider one final thought on forces which may be discouraging pastors from spending the proper amount of time in their *sacra privata*. We live in a day of the denominationally sponsored symposia, work-shops, and seminars. Understandably so. The church finds many of her called workers in trouble. She also looks for ways to renew the spirituality of her rank and file. The result has been a proliferation of church sponsored, pro-action gatherings. In the midst of these highly organized, well-intentioned, and inherently intellectualized attempts to address deeply rooted, spiritual problems, let us not forget the *sacra privata*.

Moses never attended a workshop to steady him for forty years of ministerial trials and irritations, but he did spend forty days and nights privately with God (Exodus 24:18). Jesus never attended a symposium to prepare himself for the rigors of his public ministry, but he did pray away the nights on the Judean hills privately (Mark 6:46; Luke 5:16; 6:12). Paul never attended a seminar to equip him for world evangelism; he did go to Arabia to do something mysterious (Galatians 1:17) immediately after his conversion, consulting no man or apostle.

Prayer is important. Prayer works. Yet how easy we find it to pass over this intangible solution to spiritual needs, because it seems too simplistic or because we lack the faith to carry it out! "The prayer of a righteous man is powerful and effective. Elijah was a man just like us. He prayed earnestly that it would not rain, and it did not rain on the land for three and a half years. Again he prayed, and the heavens gave rain, and the earth produced its crops" (James 5:16-18).

The Method for Personal Devotions Is Important

"To pray aright is a very difficult task and the art supreme" (*Kunst ueber alle Kuenste*),[136] said Luther.

I understand Luther's analogy to art and craft. Most artists and craftsmen spend years perfecting their native skills. Few humans with the picture or concept in their minds but without experience can, like Michelangelo, take a five meter high block of marble and produce a "David" or take copperplate, needle, ink, and rag paper like Rembrandt and pull a "Christ Healing the Sick" from the etching press. It takes time and it takes practice to make it look easy.

Prayer takes discipline. We pray in Jesus' Gethsemane spirit, "Thy will be done," always. But the question remains, "Are we disciplining ourselves to pray always?"

Meditation Means Luther's Prayer Methodology

How shall a minister pray? I favor the term meditation to explain the methodology whereby a minister combines Scripture with prayer to seek God's guidance and help.

Meditation may mean many things to people. Some may use the term meditate to refer to the act of reading a portion of Scripture. Others may call their reflection on or their contemplation of what they read in Scripture a meditation. When I use the term meditate, I am thinking specifically of the kind of praying which marked Luther's daily three hours of prayer "such as are most precious for study."

In his *A Simple Way to Pray for a Good Friend* Martin Luther instructed his barber, Peter Beskendorf, how to meditate. In this tract Luther introduced a methodology that combined the reading of Scripture with praying. His methodology consisted of a "garland of four twisted strands" which, Luther says, he wove in and through his readings. Luther explains what he means by these "four twisted strands": "I take each commandment first as a teaching, which is what it actually is, and I reflect upon what our Lord God so earnestly requires of me here. Secondly, I make out of it a reason for thanksgiving. Thirdly, a confession and fourthly, a prayer petition." This technique proved so effective that Luther told his barber, "I have learned more in one prayer than I could have obtained from much reading and thinking."

Walter Trobisch in a tract entitled *Martin Luther's Quiet Time* rearranges Luther's four thoughts. He puts them in question form.

1. What am I grateful for? (Thanksgiving)
2. What do I regret? (Confession)
3. What should I ask for? (Prayer concerns)
4. What should I do? (Action)[137]

I use Trobisch's rearrangement of Luther's "garland of four twisted strands" in my meditations, and now I know how Luther could have spent three hours a day "such as are most precious for study" in prayer. It's hard to put your Bible down after an hour's worth of meditation on its contents when you use these "four twisted strands."

You can use Luther's methodology on any portion of Scripture. For example, imagine that you are reading 1 Samuel 17, the account of David and Goliath. You relive David's experience, and then you pray over what you have read.

What do these words tell you to be grateful for? You meditate, and soon you are telling God, "I thank you that I have never had to fight a giant. I thank you that I have never had to fight for my life. I thank you that no one ever tried to take my life from me."

What do these words tell you to confess? You meditate, and then certain memories surface. "Lord, I am sorry that I remained silent when I should have condemned Mr. Smith's sin; I ran from trouble, and Mr. Smith isn't even a giant. I am sorry that I do not have the faith of David to confront the giants who seek to intimidate me."

What do these words tell you to ask God for? You think about what you are thankful for and what you have confessed, and upon reflection you tell God, "Please Lord, grant me a faith like David's so that I can meet the giants, who threaten me, head-on. Keep my enemies from physically hurting me. Give me strength to succeed when I must fight against those who war against your Word. When my efforts succeed, may people give you the glory as you received praise when David defeated Goliath."

And finally what does your reading prompt you to want to do? You have meditated on David's defeat of Goliath from the perspectives of thanksgiving, confession, and petition, bringing your thoughts to God in prayer. Now you tell God, "Bless me as I determine to confront Mr. Smith about his sin. I was afraid to say anything to him before. I know you will be with me. I will telephone him to see him tonight."

The Time and Place for Meditation

How does a minister discipline himself to meditate? Answers to this question have to revolve around two factors: time and environment.

The Lutheran Pastor gives this advice: "A minister needs his regular hours for private devotion,"[138] and a parsonage "ought to have a closet for private devotion."[139] Private is the relevant word. This often means getting up early in the morning before anyone else in the house has arisen. "Daily" and "early" is the collective advice of the ages regarding the "when" of meditation.

In addition, I offer some recent research assembled by Paul Meier, M.D., voluminous Christian author and co-host of "Psychiatry and You," a nationally syndicated television program. Meier's methodology recommends the following:

1. Go to a quiet place. Occasionally vary the pace by going out alone to a lake or stream.
2. Find a comfortable position (but preferably not lying down prone).
3. Relax your whole mind and body, including the various muscle groups.

4. Pray that the Holy Spirit will guide you into applicable truths as you read God's Word.
5. Read consecutively through the Bible, but don't place any legalistic guideline on yourself (e.g., four chapters a day, etc.).
6. When you come to a verse that jumps out at you, offers you real comfort, or otherwise confronts you with a needed behavioral change, stop and meditate on that verse or even a phrase within the verse for several minutes.
7. As you meditate on that single principle from Scripture, think of ways to appropriate personally that principle into your everyday behavior. Passively resist other unrelated thoughts and worries that intrude on your mind.[140]

In some ways Meier's techniques approach Luther's "four twisted strands" and can be interwoven or adapted. As both men stress, and as the example of our Lord underscores, the need for privacy prevails if the *sacra privata* is to be successful.

The Minister as Priest

I end this chapter, as I began it, with an anecdote involving Charles V's impact on Martin Luther's prayer life.

The date is 1529, one year earlier than the events of the Diet of Augsburg. In that year a delegation of three men, Hans Ehinger, Michael von Kaden, and Alexius Frauentraut were deputized to bear the famous "protest" of Spier to Charles V in Genoa, Italy. They secured an audience with the emperor, handed the document to him, and Frauentraut, who had become notorious for marrying a nun, told Charles V, "It is to the Supreme Judge that each one of us must render an account, and not to creatures who turn at every wind. It is better to fall into the most cruel necessity than to incur the anger of God. Our nation will obey no decrees that are based on any other foundation than the Holy Scriptures."[141]

Charles V listened and then promptly arrested the men.

I have a particular interest in this story because I am a descendant of Alexius Frauentraut, and so when I learned of this exploit I wanted to know how Luther reacted. Would Luther help my forefather, I wondered. What would the research reveal?

Research turned up a windy letter to Luther from Philip of Hesse, complaining of the men's treatment and hoping that Luther would intercede with the elector of Saxony to exploit the situation politically. Philip knew Charles needed German help to turn back the Turk. Would Luther help?[142]

"I will pray,"[143] wrote Luther to Philip.

Pray? What sort of help was that, I remember asking myself? And I have a hunch that Luther's "help" also left Philip of Hesse nonplused. Pray? I was looking for some tantalizing tidbit of politicking on the part of Luther at the least, but he would "only pray." I confess I was disappointed with Luther.

What happened to the three imprisoned men? After weeks under arrest, they managed somehow to get horses "in the middle of the night and rushed away from Genoa at full speed along a route thronged with soldiers and bandits."[144] Had Luther been spending three hours in prayer "such as are most precious for study" for these three men, interceding with God for their release? I wonder.

Luther's response of prayer as his way of helping Charles V's three prisoners seems so halfhearted. When the church faces problems and desperately needs solutions, "I will pray" hardly seems to be a helpful response to those problems. It tempts one to ask, "Is that all you are going to do? Can't you do more?"

Why should that be? Why should we be tempted to look on prayer as sort of a pie-in-the-sky solution? For one thing, prayer assaults our natural inclination to believe that all depends on our thinking and doing. For another, prayer challenges us to translate our belief in God's sovereign and providential care for his church into the appropriate behavior: trust.

Will we trust God to sort out the problems we face as pastors by bringing them to his attention? This is the priestly function of the parish pastor on behalf of his people, that before he makes attempts at problem solving he makes intercession to God, trusting, as Martin Luther did, that God will take care of things.

Making a Priestly Intercession

The adjective *priestly* does not seem to fit in with a description of the New Testament minister's function. And yet, here and there, the term sneaks into our working vocabulary. Still it causes us uneasiness.

The word *priest* implies sacrifice. The Protestant church naturally rejects the heresy which teaches that ministers sacrifice in order to complete Christ's atonement; Luther termed this teaching the "abomination" of the mass. Jesus is the priest who has "offered for all time one sacrifice for sins" (Hebrews 10:12).

As his ministers, the church has called you and me to proclaim the completeness of this sacrifice and to assure sinners that salvation has been worked for them in full (Hebrews 10:14). Publicly and privately we inform people that Christ continues in his role of high priest, pleading the case of those who put their faith in him, dispensing to them the fruit of his sacrifice, namely, the forgiveness of their sins.

When, therefore, the term *priestly* is applied to the function of the parish pastor, you and I will avoid confusing it with Christ's redemptive work. On the other hand, the

216

function of priestly intercession remains, for it applies to the pastor's role of praying on behalf of his people and for the needs and programs of the church.

As our people's pastors, you and I will intercede for them. The third verse of the hymn, "God of the Prophets, Bless the Prophet's Sons," says of ministers, "Anoint them priests. Strong intercessors, they, For pardon and for charity and peace. Ah, if with them the world might, now astray, Find in our Lord from all its woes release."[145]

Encouragements for Priestly Intercession

Intercession on behalf of my people was not one of my strong points in the early days of my ministry. It never occurred to me, in any meaningful way, that part of my function as a parish pastor was to pray for my people with any type of regularity or plan during the week. Intercessory prayer was a liturgical habit for me, something I did during the worship service on Sunday at the request of people.

My approach to intercessory prayer gradually changed. I can pinpoint no one event that made me see my role as that of a priestly intercessor, except to say that it did happen. Perhaps someone was praying for me to change my ways. At any rate, I began to intercede on behalf of people. Jill had a problem with gossip; Ron was judgmental and critical; Sally had lost her husband. I started praying for each one of them, and I kept at it. And as I started to intercede for more and more people in my prayers, the need to organize these intercessions quickly became apparent. I bought a journal to record the names of people, their needs, and how God answered my intercessions for them.

A discovery I made encouraged me, not only to continue to make these intercessions, but even to add to their number. I found that God's answers, in some cases, were sparing me the work and pain of trying to figure out solutions to some people's problems. In fact, I have seen God give such specific answers to my prayers that I no longer have trouble requesting specific items for my people in my intercessions. As answers to my prayers, I have seen troubled people admit their failings and come to me for help, and then take my advice. Yes, God had heard my prayers. I have seen parents who were wrecking their children's lives admit their failings and seek the help of the church. God heard my prayers. I have seen children, whose parents earlier would never have heard of it, enrolled in Christian Day school. God heard my prayers. I have seen people caught in sin, rebelling against God and church, humble themselves. Once again, God heard my prayers.

Some of my intercessions have gone unanswered; I continue at them. Some of them have had to wait over two years for fulfillment, and others have been answered quickly, in a matter of days or weeks. I can tell you that with accuracy because I keep track of them. My prayer log keeps track of how God has answered my intercessions. It also serves another useful purpose, for as I page through it and recall how God has acted in the past—how he has answered my intercessions on behalf of my people—I remember to give God the glory.

My past experiences have emboldened me to grow even more specific in my petitions. I am not a member of the "name it and claim it" school of enthusiasts who pray as if God had to accept their man-willed will as his own sovereign will. But, as I see problems and challenges, I do ask God for specific, detailed results. Elijah prayed *specifically* that a drought would hit Israel, and then later that it would be lifted; God heard, and he answered.

Here's an illustration of what I mean. Let's say you have a parishioner who has an annual income of $100,000 but who usually contributes only $1,000 or so a year for the Lord's work. You know that this man needs help in his stewardship life. To lead him to biblical principles of stewardship, you will want to do something specific. No, do not go and see him. First, intercede for him. Tell God about it. Ask him to change the man's heart. Ask God to give the man an evangelical perspective on his wealth. And keep at it. Who knows. You may even get a surprise phone call from the man, seeking your advice on how he can better spend his money on the Lord's work. I have had such an experience, and yes, I had been praying for such a reaction. What a grand feeling to intercede on behalf of someone who needs it, to persist in it, and then to see God open the door for a solution (Matthew 7:7)—you can't help but stand back, awestruck, and give God his due, glory.

But be cautioned. Interceding for people does not necessarily mean that God will always exempt us from the work and the pain involved in arriving at a solution. Sometimes he has given me a role in reaching the desired goal of my intercessions, and that role has cost me a lot of sleep. But, it remains a thrilling experience—having laid one's requests at heaven's throne—to see the door of opportunity opened wide for one's involvement in the solution, as if God were telling you, "All right, I approve of the plan. Get to work, and I will arrange matters in such a way that you will succeed," And, then you get to see your work end in the very success for which you had prayed.

Priestly Intercession and the Glory of God

Intercessory prayers constitute a sacrifice because in them the intercessor is offering "something" to God. You might define this "something" as the request of the prayer. But if you were to regard that as the whole sacrifice, you would be stopping short of the complete answer, for when you intercede for someone, you are offering to God, not only your request, but also your faith.

When you and I intercede for our people, God is pleased to hear our prayers because our faith produces them. Faith in Christ makes our prayers acceptable to God. As such, our intercessions constitute worship. You will recognize how this facet of pastoral life fits into the prime directive that God is to be glorified in all of our activities. Through your act of interceding for your people or for your parish plans you are glorifying God through your faithful petitions.

Mister minister, this is thrilling stuff! How wonderful it is to know that God *wants* our intercessions, that he *promises* to answer us, and that when we petition him in faith, he is *pleased* to accept our worshipful concerns. Of course, we propose, and God disposes; God willing, he will answer as we have petitioned.

Be the people's priest; intercede for them. Be happy in the knowledge that you are making God happy as you besiege him with your priestly mediations for your people and your plans. As you see your role as priestly intercessor grow and develop, your vision of soli Deo gloria will fill you with a deepening sense of grace. You will find a strength, not from within yourself, but from God, working through your prayers to encourage you onward in your ministrations. You will feel a boldness to do and to dare things in the name of Christ, because you have a record of answered petitions that encourages you in your belief that this same glorious God will so attend you in the future.

And most important of all. Every time you petition God on behalf of one of his redeemed children, you are waving the blood-red banner of his Son in victory over Satan. You are signaling to God that you side with him in the battle over the souls of human beings, and that you appreciate his grace which has won the day.

As you make your petitions for his redeemed children, you will better appreciate this grace of God in Christ Jesus, who mediated salvation for sinners without their request, but with their best interests in mind—for this is what you are doing when you intercede for others. Your intercessions imitate Christ's unsolicited, gracious attention in that you mark the behavior and needs of your people and, without their solicitation, you pray on their behalf. In this way you become, as Luther would put it, a little Christ, and you have come to understand better than most why God is glorified: in our great need, when we were not seeking God's help, he came unsolicited to our aid and sent his Son, Jesus, to mediate our salvation. It's thrilling to copy this attitude in our work.

Summary

1. For a pastor to have a regular, private devotional life is important, because he always needs to communicate with his pastor, Jesus Christ. Pastors need to maintain a two-way conversation with Jesus, in which they allow him to speak to them (Scripture), and they talk to him (prayer).
2. The average pastor does not spend enough time in prayer. A pastor may be shortchanging his prayer life because (1) he is lazy, or (2) he believes prayer to be unimportant, or (3) he believes that reading the Bible substitutes for praying, or (4) he believes that praying too much is an extreme to be avoided, or (5) he lacks a proper relationship with God, or (6) he emphasizes intellectual solutions for what are essentially spiritual problems.
3 Luther's meditation methodology involved reading Scripture and then composing free prayers over what he read. These prayers centered on the topics of thanksgiving, confession, intercessions, and action. Meditation should be private and regular.
4. Parish pastors have a priestly function in that they intercede on behalf of their parishioners through their prayers. As pastors get to know their people, they will see their people's problems, and, unsolicited, they will

take these concerns to God. As they practice this priestly intercession, they will grow all the more appreciative
of the way that God graciously sent his Son to work salvation for the human race. This strengthens their resolve to do all things soli Deo gloria.

Advice

1. I had written that the discipline needed for meditation
   usually revolves around the factors of time and environment (p. 213). Consider also the matter of language. As I started to spend more time in meditation, I
   discovered how easy it was to let my mind wander as I
   read. As a solution I switched to the Vulgate. You may
   elect to read the Bible in German, Greek, Hebrew, or in
   a language that is new to you. The point is that by doing
   so you will find yourself forced to dwell more on the
   thoughts of the text, simply because you must concentrate more on the foreign words. It took me more
   than two years to read through the Gospels of Matthew
   and Luke using Jerome's translation and Luther's "four
   twisted strands" (p. 212), but the combination of these
   two techniques beats any other method I had previously
   employed.
2. As a variation on maintaining a prayer journal or log,
   consider using your parish's member directory. Set aside
   thirty minutes every Saturday evening, and pray through
   a portion of your membership alphabetically, noting intercessory concerns. Do this the night before services
   and see if it also doesn't put you in a pastoral mood to
   meet the people.
3. On page 189 of *Fallen Shepherds Scattered Sheep* F. LaGard
   Smith encourages ministers to take sabbaticals from
   their churches, as a means to recharge spiritual batteries.
   He cites the example of Christ, advocating that such

sabbaticals should avoid academic pursuits and be a time of quiet reflection.

Endnotes

[119] Plass, *What Luther Says*, 3:1103.

[120] Pope, "Opinion Poll of Select Protestant Clergymen of the Greater Milwaukee Area," 5.

[121] Ibid., 8.

[122] Ibid., 11.

[123] Ibid., 12.

[124] Ibid., 16.

[125] Ibid., 18.

[126] Ibid., 19.

[127] Ibid., passim.

[128] Ibid., 13.

[129] Schuetze and Habeck, *The Shepherd under Christ* [Emphasis added].

[130] Jay E. Adams, *The Pastoral Life* (Grand Rapids: Baker Book House, 1974), 23.

[131] Ibid., 23 [Emphasis added].

[132] G. H. Gerberding, *The Lutheran Pastor* (Philadelphia: Lutheran Publication Society, 1902), 196.

[133] Ibid., 195.

[134] Martin E. Lehman, *Luther and Prayer* (Milwaukee, Wisconsin: Northwestern Publishing House, 1985), 5.

[135] F. LaGard Smith, *Fallen Shepherds Scattered Sheep*, 184,185.

[136] Plass, *What Luther Says*, 2:1088.

[137] Walter Trobisch, *Martin Luther's Quiet Time* (Downers Grove, Illinois: InterVarsity Press, 1975), 8.

[138] Gerberding, *The Lutheran Pastor*, 197.

[139] Ibid., 199.

[140] Paul Meier, *Meditating for Success* (Grand Rapids, Michigan: Baker Book House, 1985), 59,60.

[141] Theodore Graebner, *The Story of the Augsburg Confession* (St. Louis: Concordia Publishing House, 1929), 68.

[142] *Dr. Martin Luther's Saemmtlich Schriften*, Vol. XXIa (St. Louis: Concordia Publishing House, 1887), 1483.

[143] Ibid., 1487.

[144] Graebner, *The Story of the Augsburg Confession*, 69.

[145] *The Lutheran Hymnal* (St. Louis: Concordia Publishing House, 1941), 483.

CHAPTER 13
TAKE UP
THE CROSS

The Ministry in America Is in Turmoil

Resignations are emptying pulpits across our country. Like other denominations, my church body, the Wisconsin Evangelical Lutheran Synod, has experienced the turmoil created by pastoral disillusionment and resignations. At last count thirteen of the seventy college classmates who entered the seminary with me in 1972 have, for one reason or another, left the parish ministry.

Morale among the clergy continues to plummet. Edward Bratcher cites a survey of 4,665 Protestant ministers that indicated that fifty-eight percent felt that the work of the church seemed futile or ineffectual.[146] Burnout has turned into a ministerial phenomenon and preoccupation. Bratcher writes: "Reverend Roy Oswald, a behavioral scientist and authority on clergy burnout, believes that one out of every four clergy is burned out and another twenty-five percent are under great stress and may be on their way to burnout."[147]

Burnout among ministers has grown so acute and wide-spread that an entire industry has arisen to deal with the problem. Books, seminars, and workshops, intended to combat clergy stress and to reverse the escalating trend of resignations, are found everywhere.

I am troubled, however, by some of the advice that is being offered as a solution to the current problems of the clergy and by the tone in which it is given. In much of it I detect a subliminal whine which seeks to convince us pastors, "You have it tough, tougher than any generation of pastors before you." I am concerned that, in attempting to combat the weariness and stress of working directly with sinners (Chapter 7), we are convincing ourselves to accept an extreme interpretation of the ministry's "jars of clay" description (2 Corinthians 4:7), an interpretation which wants to turn us into softies.

The Ministry Has Always Been a Tough Place

The apostle Paul was no fool, and he was no wimp; he was a self-confessed warrior.

In his second letter to the Corinthians Paul boasted of his sufferings, relating how, in the appointed course of his ministrations, he had experienced everything from whippings to sneak attacks by bandits (2 Corinthians 11:16-33). In bold strokes he described the nature of his service to God as that of a soldier engaged in spiritual warfare, and he used that same metaphor to encourage young Timothy: "You then, my son, be strong in the grace that is in Christ Jesus. . . . Endure hardship with us like a good soldier of Christ Jesus (2 Timothy 2:1,3).

Anyone who desires to become a minister of Christ must, therefore, expect to have it tough. It can be no other way. But, you should not read that to mean that your calling sentences you to a tough life where you are out on your own without any help. Reread Paul's exhortation to Timothy. As he describes the tough conditions of ministry, he also points Timothy to its buttress and underpinnings, the "grace that is in Christ Jesus." That which makes God so glorious, that for which we give him the glory, his grace—so free, so full, so lavish (Exodus 34:6,7)—also will keep strong those who minister in his name, no matter under what conditions they work. How glorious is this ministry, in that the message it proclaims—the grace of God in Christ Jesus—also becomes its spiritual food, a spiritual food that sustains those who are called to tough out its responsibilities!

There Is an Inherent Tension in the Ministry

Have you ever noticed how some of your unchurched neighbors, when they spot you walking down the sidewalk, beat a path to the opposite side of the street in a not-so-discreet attempt to avoid meeting you face to face? Perhaps you have also encountered this same phenomenon in the form of a parishioner who pretends not to see you and goes out of his way to avoid you. You can allow these incidents to make you feel like a pariah, but I would ask you to try and understand why people do this. Most often they have nothing against you personally. If you were the church's janitor and you ran into them on the street, they would cheerfully greet you and ask you how you were, or they might use the occasion to complain about the condition of the lavatories. But you are not the janitor; you are the pastor. And when people see you striding down the street or pushing a cart towards them in aisle three, "Sugar, Cooking Oil, and Flour," most feel intimidated by your presence.

Yes, it is true. You make people feel uncomfortable. A tension exists between you and your parishioners; they feel it, and so do you. And, this tension often keeps you from acting like yourself when you are faced with the dilemma of correcting or criticizing people.

Easter has arrived, and you have produced what you consider to be one of your finest worship services and sermons. You are looking forward to conducting and participating in an inspiring service. But, you begin to be concerned when you spot Mrs. Smith, your very worst organist, slide into position on the console bench. You stand in the sacristy, fretting, and then you hear her botch the prelude. Then, to ice the matter, she manages somehow to hammer out the wrong melody for the processional hymn. Your service is spoiled already. You are beside yourself. What do you do? How do you act?

Do you (1) rake Mrs. Smith over the coals immediately after the service, (2) wait until Easter Monday to do it, (3) delegate the task to an elder who would relish the assignment, or (4) say nothing to her except to wish her, "Happy Easter?" Easy choice, right?

A tension does exist between us and our parishioners which tends, on the one hand, to keep us from acting completely like ourselves, and on the other hand, creates a certain distance between US and THEM. Depending on the situation, you may believe that this tension is good or bad; it may tug at you gently, or it may make you feel that you are ready to snap like a stretched-out rubber band.

The tension originates in our call to function as God's representative. When you meet people, you know whom you represent, and you must act accordingly; people also know this. Consequently, when parishioners spot you, or you spot them, a certain tension to be on good behavior is felt by both parties, and if one or both parties does not particularly welcome this feeling, one or the other will look for a place to hide.

You have, undoubtedly, felt such tension when you sought to avoid a situation much like the one I described with my imaginary organist, Mrs. Smith. You may have wanted to avoid the tension inherent in that pastor-parishioner situation, especially if you felt as if you wanted to act like someone other than God's representative.

Representing and modeling the name of Christ publicly and professionally makes the ministry a tough call.

There Is an Inherent Hostility to the Ministry

What did Adam and Eve do after they had eaten of the forbidden fruit and heard their Creator strolling in the garden? They hid.

So your neighbor or your parishioner may also want to avoid you because they have sinned against God and the sight of you troubles or agitates their conscience. Or people may pale at the sight of you or grow angry, not because they are upset with you, but because they are upset with your "boss."

The sinful human nature harbors an inherently hostile attitude towards God (Romans 8:7). Sin has created in human nature an inbred, natural loathing towards God and his will (Genesis 6:5; Romans 3:10-18). And you and I naturally get caught up in this conflict since we are called to represent God. Ministers, as Oates correctly points out, symbolically represent God's power.[148] Ministers, consequently, pose convenient, visible targets for people who really carry a chip on their shoulder against God, and this may explain why you and I find ourselves caught in the middle of many tough situations.

Remember when the three stooges, Moe, Larry, and Curly dressed up for a gala social event? How did their meal usually end? Right, in a pie fight. And why? Because an innocent by-stander, caught standing between an airborne pie and its intended target, was hit and, *voile*, took it personally. So you and I, in a sense, also find ourselves standing between the throwers and their intended target, and in this case the target turns out to be God.

This phenomenon should come as no surprise, since Jesus outlined it 2000 years ago to the first New Testament ministers: "He who listens to you listens to me; he who rejects you rejects me; but he who rejects me rejects him who sent me (Luke 10:16). And Jesus added the prediction: "No servant is greater than his master. If they persecuted me, they will persecute you also" (John 15:20).

But you may protest, "This should not be; if these people are really angry with God, why should I get it?" But I will say, "People can only hit what they see." So when you are invited to that celebration and the host introduces you to that group of strangers seated in the living room, and a painfully brief but eloquent silence follows, force yourself to avoid taking the matter personally. You represent the greatest power in the universe, and some live in rebellion of it and fear it, and others just plain hate it. And because you represent it, the sight of you causes many a countenance to fall (Genesis 4:6). It's always been that way with God's ministers.

Ministers Have Always Had It Tough

Much has been said and written about how difficult the ministry has become in today's church. Yes, we minister under tough conditions. People will always feel uptight around us, and we will feel a persistent tension as we work with people. People will also take out their hostilities towards God on us because we, as his representatives, make convenient targets.

But our ministries could be worse. Much worse.

No parishioner who disliked one of my sermons has ever slapped me in the face; Zedekiah, son of Kenannah slapped Micaiah in the face for his prophetic utterance (1 Kings 22:24). People have said some nasty things to me over the years, but no one has ever threatened me with death or physically roughed me up; a mob once greeted Jeremiah's words with death threats (Jeremiah 26:8), and on a different occasion the prophet's enemies deposited him a mud-filled hole (Jeremiah 38:6). Unfair words and actions have been directed against me on numerous occasions when I have had to point out people's sins, but those frays never cost me my head; John's fray with Herod did (Matthew 14:10).

I have yet to face some terrible form of persecution. I have not experienced jeers, flogging, or stoning, been cut by a sword or sawed in two. I have never been deported to a desert or a mountain or forced to live in a cave or a hole (Hebrews 11:36-38).

Have you?

Are we not better off than the majority of our biblical or historical counterparts? When you get right down to it, we should consider ourselves blessed to minister in this age of relative peace and tranquillity towards the Christian clergy. How joyful it should make us feel that we can set out for church services every Sunday morning with nothing more serious on our minds than a concern that we will remember our sermons, rather than having to worry, instead, whether the authorities will be waiting for us at the church doors to arrest us because our doctrine or practice does not meet with the approval of the government. How our biblical and historical counterparts were persecuted, even martyred for their faith! Yes, we labor in a very tough profession, but how little we have suffered by comparison.

Weaklings Who Become Strong

The Apostle Paul, who could boast of his capacity to endure hardships, explained where he found the strength to do so. He confessed his deficiencies and thereby was made strong: "For when I am weak, then I am strong" (2 Corinthians 12:10). Paul was made strong inasmuch as he was willing to admit his weaknesses and to find his strength in the grace of God in Christ. God told him: "My grace is sufficient for you, for my power is made perfect in weakness" (2 Corinthians 12:9). By faith Paul became strong: "Therefore I will boast all the more gladly about my weaknesses, so that Christ's power may rest on me. That is why, for Christ's sake, I delight in weaknesses, in insults, in hardships, in persecutions, in difficulties. For when I am weak, then am I strong" (2 Corinthians 9:9,10).

Every hardship, every trouble, every tough situation which the gospel puts us in, gives us the opportunity to learn anew the power and the strength inherent in God's grace. When tough situations reveal our weaknesses and our dependency upon God, the grace of God never looks better or richer. When people problems have rubbed our nerves raw or when failed plans have cost us sleep or when we feel unappreciated or forsaken, we will retreat into the grace of God. And we will experience new energy as our faith affirms what makes God so glorious, his grace . . . his grace which caused God to send his Son to save us from our sins, a mercy completely unsolicited. We really do enjoy the glories of God's grace; our names are written in heaven.

And once you have retreated into the glories of God's grace, what happens then? Then, in spite of the troubles, the problems, the frustrations, you feel the drive to go on, to persevere. Then you know that God's blessings rest upon you, that he loves you, and that he appreciates the trouble you go through to advance the glory of his grace. When the tough business of the ministry has once again opened your eyes to the riches of God's grace, you find the necessary strength. How good, indeed, it is to glory in God's grace!

The Ministry Is a Cross

Do you know how many variations of the cross exist? Hundreds.[149] Each one of these crosses, while based on the one on which Christ hung, has its own personality or peculiarity. So, too, it is with the crosses which Jesus says his followers must pick up and carry. These exist, not in the hundreds, but in the untold millions—as many, in fact, as those who have ever put their faith in the One who hung on the center cross on Calvary and through devotion to that One have endured trouble for his name. The individual circumstances of life fashion each one of these crosses differently from the next, and yet all are patterned after the Calvary original in terms of self-denial. Jesus said, "If anyone would come after me, he must deny himself and take up his cross and follow me" (Matthew 16:24). The ministry which aims to promote Christ crucified can only be defined as a cross in the truest sense of self-denial.

Pick up the Real Cross

Every minister who would "follow" (Matthew 16:24) Christ must reconcile himself to the inevitable fact that he, as it were, has become a Simon from Cyrene and that he must shoulder his ministry as a cross. The word cross teaches us explicitly that the ministry is not supposed to be easy. Those who complain about the minister's cross need to remember that Jesus termed it so, and that while he plainly used the word cross as a metaphor, the trouble, yes, the stress which comes from shouldering it goes hand in hand with the message of grace.

That leads me to wonder how many ministers, in these days of affluence and plenty in America, have dropped their crosses because the central beliefs of their ministries have turned out to be counterfeits. The heroes of faith, the biblical and historical ones, endured great hardships because the crosses of their ministries were extensions of the gospel which proclaims salvation from hell. Consequently, the minister who views his life, his work, and his identity from this same otherworldly perspective can put up with the trials and tribulations which result from advancing such a theology. As Paul said, "But whatever was to my profit I now consider loss for the sake of Christ. What is more, I consider everything a loss compared to the surpassing greatness of knowing Christ Jesus my Lord, *for whose sake I have lost all things*. I consider them rubbish, that I may gain Christ and be found in him, not having a righteousness of my own that comes from the law, but that which is through faith in Christ—the righteousness that comes from God and is by faith. I want to know Christ and the *power of his resurrection and the fellowship of sharing in his sufferings*, becoming like him in his death, and so, somehow, to attain to the resurrection from the dead." (Philippians 3:7-11).

Is it any wonder then that some want no share in the rigors of the ministry—the long, unpredictable hours, the tension of working with people in their most sensitive area (the soul), the apparent lack of accomplishments and appreciation—because the cross they carried bore a false christ on its arms? Those who would seek to save society, but not souls, by the preaching of some kind of gospel in the name of some kind of christ, will grow disenchanted with the ministry and its glorious legacy since they have denied its historic Christocentricity and the sola's of the Reformation, *sola fide* (a man is saved by faith alone), *sola gratia* (man has been saved by God's grace alone), and *sola scriptura* (all teaching is drawn from God's inerrant Scripture alone).

Christ's call to pick up the cross forms a challenge to faith; it challenges the minister to preach Christ crucified faithfully (1 Corinthians 2:2). He who lifts up the true cross, accordingly accepts its burdens, sets his gaze on the distant, gathering clouds of eternity, and like a good soldier of God pushes forward *soli Deo gloria* with a song of victory in his heart.

Pick up the Cross

"The purpose of my future parish ministry is to the glory of the Triune Lord—through training those he's already gained and witnessing to others he hasn't—I mean this from my heart."[150] May God grant to us the heart to feel clearly the glory of God's grace, as evidenced by this seminarian's explanation of the purpose of his future calling.

Open your eyes wide and discover anew the reflected glory of the Christian ministry. What a joy it is to believe that Christ has forgiven us our sins; what a privilege it is that his church has called us to proclaim that good news.

Promote the grace of God, which "denotes that which makes God impressive."[151] Preach Christ crucified to the salvation of sinners and to the ultimate glory of God, and experience a growing sense of accomplishment, a driving power to persevere in your ministry, a deepening sense of dedication, an increasing desire to make personal and professional improvements, and feel your heart grow happier. Pick up your cross, and glorify your God.

"There is a refreshment of achievement in glorifying God with which nothing else can be compared."[152]

Summary

1. Burnout has hit the ministry, resulting in many resignations and leaving many of those who remain discouraged.
2. The ministry has always been a tough place. There is an inherent tension in it because the pastor has a call to function publicly as God's representative. At the same time there is an inherent hostility towards the ministry because many people feel hostile toward God and take out their feelings on his called representatives. Retreating into the grace of God in Christ Jesus remains the only way for weaklings to become strong, as Paul reminded the Corinthians.
3. The ministry constitutes a real cross in terms of self-denial. When the pressures of pastoral life become great and when the troubles of pastoral life increase, those

235

who have emptied the cross of its salvific worth will find the ministry not worth the trouble. Christ's call to pick up the cross challenges ministers to preach the gospel faithfully. Glory in the grace of the Christ crucified.

Advice

1. I remember a pastor telling me that he had written letters of resignation to his congregation twice, only to throw them away. He didn't say what had brought him to that point, but I received the distinct impression that the mere act of writing the letters somehow made him feel better. If you were to compose such a letter of resignation from the call you presently serve, would it make you feel better to put into print your frustrations and disappointments, to confront yourself with these feelings, rather than just keeping them bottled up within you?

2. Write a second letter. This time compose a letter that you would want your descendants to find among your effects 100 years after your death. Tell them the difficulties of ministering at the close of the 20th century, but also relate how glorious was your ministry and why you never gave it up.

Endnotes

[146] Bratcher, The Walk-on-Water Syndrome, 9.

[147] Ibid.

[148] See the second chapter of his book, The Christian Pastor, "The Symbolic Power of the Pastor," 65-95.

[149] F. R. Webber, Church Symbolism (Cleveland: J. H. Hansen Publishers, 1938), 99, points out that there are over 400 different variations on the cross.

[150] Nathan R. Pope, "Survey of Students of Wisconsin Lutheran Seminary, 5.

[151] See Chapter 2 in this writing for Kittel's definition of *kabod*.

[152] Adams, *Back to the Blackboard*, 36.

Index of Scripture References

Index

INDEX